Children of the Ice

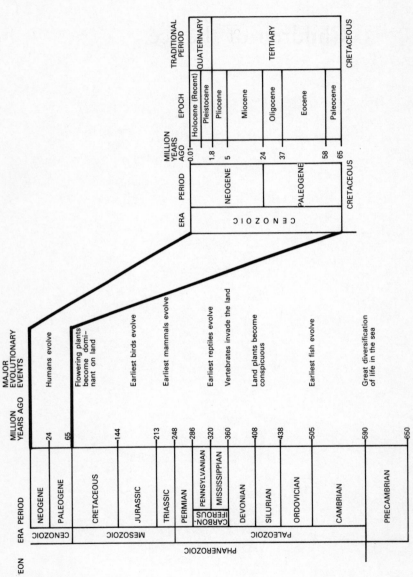

Landmarks in the Evolution of Life

Source: Adapted from data in *Extinction*, Steven M. Stanley, San Francisco, Scientific American Library, 1987

Children of the Ice

Climate and Human Origins

John and Mary Gribbin

Basil Blackwell

Copyright © John and Mary Gribbin 1990

First published 1990
Reprinted 1990

Basil Blackwell Ltd
108 Cowley Road, Oxford OX4 1JF, UK

Basil Blackwell Inc.
3 Cambridge Center
Cambridge, Massachusetts 02142, USA

British Library Cataloguing in Publication Data

A CIP catalogue record for this book is available from the British Library.

Library of Congress Cataloging in Publication Data

Gribbin, John R.
Children of the ice: climate and human origins / John and Mary Gribbin.
   p. cm.
Includes bibliographical references.
ISBN 0–631–16817–6
1. Man—Origins. 2. Human evolution. 3. Climatic changes.
I. Gribbin, Mary. II. Title.
GN281.G739   1990
573.2—dc20   89–17532   CIP

Typeset in 11 on 12 pt Sabon
by Photographics, Honiton, Devon
Printed in Great Britain by T. J. Press Ltd, Padstow, Cornwall

Contents

Acknowledgements

Many of the themes developed in this book were first aired by John Gribbin as a BBC Radio Four series, 'Children of the Ice', in 1988. As with our previous book, *The One Per Cent Advantage*, the exposition of these ideas has benefited from discussions with the producer of the radio version, Michael Bright.

Introduction

Why are we here? How is it that human beings are among the more successful forms of life on Earth today? There are many answers to these questions, depending on the prejudices of the person you address them to. A cosmologist might tell you about the Big Bang in which our Universe was born, and the way in which the chemical elements of which our bodies are composed were cooked in stars. An evolutionary biologist might talk of natural selection, and survival of the fittest. Both have a point. But we blame the weather – or rather, if we are going to be strictly accurate about these things, the changing climate.

Mankind has emerged during an interval of unusual and rapidly changing climate on Earth, conditions which put adaptability and intelligence at a premium, and which pushed one species of African ape out of the woods and on to the path to world domination. But then, what were those apes doing in the trees in the first place? They owed *their* existence to a far more dramatic environmental change which took place roughly 65 million years ago. If it hadn't been for the death of the dinosaurs, mammals might never have been more than inconspicuous creatures, occupying small-animal niches in the ecology and scurrying about in the undergrowth. And what killed the dinosaurs? Almost certainly, bad weather.

Mammals had actually been around for more than a hundred million years before the abrupt (geologically speaking) end to the era of the dinosaurs. The two kinds of animal can hardly be said to have been in conflict. That was a long period of climatic calm and constancy, in which the dinosaurs ruled the roost because they were well adapted to existing conditions, and no new variations on the evolutionary theme got much of a look in.

We certainly cannot make any kind of a case that our ancestors were any more intelligent than their dinosaur contemporaries. The traditional picture of the lumbering, stupid dinosaur with a huge body and tiny brain tells only part of the story. Many dinosaurs *were* big and stupid; many more, though, were smaller, agile and with respectably large brains for their body weight. They may even have been warm-blooded. There were dinosaur equivalents of hunters like the tiger and the lion, as well as dinosaur equivalents of grazers like the hippopotamus and the elephant. They weren't beaten in the evolutionary stakes by smarter mammals, but were wiped out by environmental catastrophe – a change in the rules of the game.

It is a sign of how successful dinosaurs were, in their own time, that they were actually a *younger* variation on the theme of life than mammals. Mammal-like reptiles existed *before* dinosaurs came on the scene, and they were displaced by the dinosaurs. We are descended from the *ancestors* of dinosaurs.

And before that? Like the character in the *Mikado*, we can trace our ancestry 'back to a protoplasmal primordial atomic globule. Consequently [our] family pride is something inconceivable.' In this book, however, we don't want to go that far. In order to make our story manageable, we have to start quite late in the evolution of life on Earth, when our ancestors had already emerged from the sea on to the land. This is not merely a narrative convenience, since life on land has been subject to much more in the way of vicissitudes and changing environmental conditions than life in the seas ever was. That is a major reason why evolution on land has proceeded so swiftly in the past few hundred million years, and why we are here to speculate on our origins.

It is a story full of death and destruction, and before we begin the tale proper we should set the scene by discussing some of the relevant agents of destruction. Like a horror movie, this should be viewed as entertainment; the prospect of some natural catastrophe wiping human life out tomorrow is about on a par with the prospect of being attacked by a mad chain-saw murderer on the way home from the movies. But the difference is that our story is true. Not even the names have been changed ...

1

Dead as the Dodo

The story of life on Earth might better be described as the story of death on Earth. Far more species of plant and animal life than those that are alive today are now extinct, wiped from the face of the Earth because changing environmental conditions made their lifestyles untenable, destroying the ecological niches that they inhabited. And yet we are, by definition, descended from survivors. We can trace our ancestry back in an unbroken line to single-celled creatures swimming in the seas of our planet some three and a half thousand million years ago. Before that, the picture becomes more hazy, but the basic similarity of the life processes in all living things, involving molecules such as DNA, RNA and proteins, suggests that we are all descended from some common ancestor, a collection of molecules that first learned the trick of self-replication.

Replication, of course, is what life is all about. Living things make copies of themselves. But those copies are not necessarily *exact* replicas of their parents, and that is why life on Earth has been able to evolve and adapt to changing environmental pressures. In each generation, there is a variety of individuals, even within the confines of one particular species. Those individuals that do best – the ones that 'fit' their environment – leave more descendants behind, so that the characteristics that make individuals successful are preferentially passed on to later generations. As long as the environment is essentially unchanging, much of this evolution by natural selection simply makes a species better suited to its ecological niche – monkeys become better adapted to a life in the trees; birds develop ever better wings, and so on. But when the environment changes, many superbly adapted individuals, and even whole species, are wiped out, because the conditions they are adapted to no longer exist. If all trees disappeared, for example, monkeys would have to learn a new way of life or die. In such circumstances, whether the change is rapid or gradual, the pattern of life is altered. Some species die; descendants of other species come under new selection pressures, and evolve accordingly. Given new opportunities, descendants of the survivors diversify, and new species arise to fill the new ecological niches. From a human perspective, the story of life on Earth is very much one of change and adaptation – a series of changes and adaptations that have led to us – with a great deal of death (of other forms of life) along the way.

Evolution at work

We touched briefly on the way evolution works, at the level of the molecule of life, DNA, in our previous book, *The One Per Cent Advantage*. Some people do still worry about the whole business of Darwinian evolution, however, as questions we have been asked by readers of that book make clear. The main worry that arises in people's minds concerns complexity – how can something as complicated as a human being (or an eye, or the echo-location 'radar' of a bat) have arisen, they ask 'by chance'? The question is based on a misunderstanding of how evolution works. True, there is an element of chance, in the sense that any small change in the hereditary material – the DNA – that we pass on to our children may be a random alteration of the genetic code. But even this change can only start out from the version of the code the parents carry. If you liken the code to a 'recipe' for, say, a human being, it is equivalent to a fat encyclopedia written in our familiar alphabet. The random change that is part of the evolutionary process may amount to altering the spelling of a few words in that encyclopedia – not, in going from one generation to the next, to producing a new, encyclopedia-length recipe, by jumbling up all the letters of the alphabet at random. And, equally important, there is no chance in the vital element of *selection* that follows, with individuals that fit the environment doing well while those that are poorly suited to their surroundings do badly. It is not as if you took a huge tub of chemicals and stirred them up, waiting for some lucky chance to bring together, in working order, the constituents of a living human being, or even a living cell. Evolution proceeds step by step, each tiny step building on a pre-existing, working system (real chance, or luck, does come into the equation for the origin of the first living molecule(s), but there was enough time available, and enough molecules around, for life itself to have emerged in this way, genuinely as a result of a lucky accident). The important point is that evolution has had an almost inconceivably long time to work with: at least three and a half *billion* years, since life appeared in the oceans.

Richard Dawkins, in his superb book *The Blind Watchmaker*, puts this in perspective – and also, incidentally, gives the numbers which show how the first living molecules could indeed have appeared by chance. In the span of a few thousand years, at most, people have produced the entire variety of modern dogs from an ancestral wolf species. In each generation, individual people have picked out the dogs they like best (for whatever reason) and used them as breeding stock. This, in a sense, is 'unnatural' selection, since it operates in accordance with human whim. But, to a dog, human beings are part of 'the environment', and the process is exactly the same as natural selection. It takes us from wolf to chihuahua in a couple of thousand years. Dawkins suggests that you think of this as a 'distance', equivalent to a single human pace. On that scale, how far would you have to walk along the evolutionary road to go back to the start of evolution on Earth? All the way from London to Baghdad. Evolution has had a *lot* of time to play with. If you are still worried about the details, we recommend Dawkins's book to set your mind at ease (indeed, even if you are not worried about evolution, we still recommend *The Blind Watchmaker*, as the best non-technical guide to the whole story). Our aim is not to persuade any doubters that evolution works, but to use the fact of evolution, combined with evidence that the environment of our planet has changed dramatically while life has evolved, to explain how it is that a species of intelligent ape descended from tree-climbing primates should be sitting here wondering about such things, while the dinosaurs, who ruled the Earth for more than 150 million years, have been wiped from the face of the planet.

There are other perspectives. There are single-celled organisms around, scarcely different from our ancestors of three-billion-plus years ago. From their perspective, the story of life on Earth is one of continuity and stability. *Their* way of life has not been threatened by any environmental changes, and they are superbly adapted – superbly fitted – to a particular ecological niche. The complexity of multi-celled plant and animal life is simply a curious and incidental by-product of their success.

But, of course, that is not our perspective, and single-celled life forms (which, in terms of longevity, are undoubtedly the most successful living forms on 'our' planet) will not get much of a mention in the rest of this book. Indeed, life in the oceans scarcely gets a look in, even though for three billion years the story of life on Earth *was* the story of life in the oceans. Plants only colonized the land a little over 400 million years ago, rapidly followed by creatures such as millipedes, mites and the first insects. Trees and forests had evolved by about 370 million years ago, and the earliest amphibians, our direct ancestors, crawled ashore at about the same time. That is where we choose to begin our story of the changing environmental conditions that made some of the descendants of those amphibian inhabitants of the Paleozoic Era into human beings. But we ought to set the scene by digressing, briefly, to explain how anybody knows what was going on 370 million years ago, or what life forms lived when during the subsequent history of the Earth, and how the environment did change.

The record in the rocks

Fossils are the key to understanding the story of life on Earth. When some living things (plants or animals) die, their remains fall into the ooze of the sea-bed, the mud near a lake, or some other place where the pieces can be covered by inorganic material and buried before some passing creature eats them. As more sediments are deposited above the remains, the lower layers are squeezed tight. Eventually, geological forces may mould the sediments into rock, and that rock may carry the imprint of the once-living remains, fossils that are now made of stone but which still bear the shape of the organic remains that fell into the sediments millions of years before. *Most* organic remains are *not* preserved in this way, but just a few are.

Such stony copies of living things have been known for hundreds of years – Leonardo da Vinci, for example, remarked on them in the fifteenth century, and fossils were a cause of great debate, and puzzlement, among the natural philosophers of the seventeenth century. Ideas developed slowly, but a key step was taken late in the eighteenth century by the English surveyor William Smith, who saw the layers of fossil-bearing strata revealed by new canals and coal mining activity. He realized that different strata contain different, distinctive types of fossil remains, and that rocks of the same age from different parts of Britain (and, we now know, the rest of the world) can be identified by the characteristic fossils they contain.

In most places, older rocks lie beneath more recently formed rocks, and preserve traces of the fauna and flora of their times. This gave paleontologists and geologists a relative timescale, and was a key influence on Charles Darwin as he developed his theory of evolution in the nineteenth century. But it was only in the present century that physicists provided geologists with an accurate clock that could be used to calibrate the geological timescale.

When the geological timescale was first constructed, no dates on it were anything better than guesses. The timescale was divided up, like a geological calendar, into different intervals; but the division was largely on the basis of changes in the fossil record. In some layers of rock, there is very little difference between the kinds of fossil found in one layer and those found in the layer above. In other cases, many types of fossil that are present in the lower layer are nowhere to be seen in the upper layer, and 'new' fossils, representing different forms of life, have emerged to take their place (or emerge more gradually as the geologist looks at successively younger layers). The boundaries between geological intervals very often coincide with interesting changes in the pattern of development of life on Earth, precisely because those interesting changes in the fossil record are used as the markers for geological intervals.

In the twentieth century, these geological intervals have been assigned dates, thanks to the development of radioactive dating techniques. Most things contain traces of radioactive elements, and the strength of the radioactivity of a particular sample of rock (granite, perhaps) decreases as time passes in a regular and now well-understood way. By measuring the radioactivity of a sample of old rock, physicists can calculate how long it has been since that rock was laid down. The figures are not absolutely precise, and slightly different techniques yield slightly different ages, which is why one book may say that the age of the dinosaurs ended 65 million years ago, while another gives the date as 67 million years ago, and a third, more cautiously, refuses to give dates but says only that the dinosaurs died out at the end of the Cretaceous Period (which really is not much help, since one definition of 'the end of the Cretaceous' is 'when the dinosaurs died out'). The dates we shall use here are largely taken from Steven Stanley's book *Extinction*.

Geological time is divided into different slices according to the nature of changes in the fossil record. Big changes – massive extinctions of life – mark the boundaries of more important intervals; little changes – the death of a few species – mark the boundaries of minor subdivisions. Everything that happened before 590 million years ago (590 Myr) is called the Precambrian, and this seven-eighths or so of the history of our planet is largely a blank area as far as our knowledge of life is concerned. Good fossils are only found from later strata (which is why the boundary is set at 590 Myr). The eon we live in, from the Precambrian to the present, is called the Phanerozoic, and this is divided into three eras, the Paleozoic (from 590 Myr to 248 Myr), the Mesozoic (from 248 Myr to 65 Myr) and the Cenozoic (from 65 Myr onwards). Smaller intervals within eras are called periods, and their names will crop up from time to time in our story. The first period of the Paleozoic Era of the Phanerozoic Eon is called the Cambrian – which is why everything earlier is called the Precambrian. Periods are divided into epochs, and epochs into ages, but such subtle distinctions will hardly bother us at all. What we are interested in is why there should have been times, especially at the boundaries between periods, when many forms of life went extinct together. What were the catastrophic changes in the environment that brought doom to the dinosaurs 65 million years ago (thereby opening the way for the rise of the mammals, our own class of animal), and which caused similar extinctions in the more distant geological past?

All things must pass

It's important that fossil hunters don't get *too* carried away by the appearance of gaps in the fossil record. By its very nature, the process of fossilization provides an imperfect record of the evolution of life, and some of the gaps in that record are there not because species died out but because their remains happen not to have been preserved. This is important in two ways. First, because we have to be sure that many different species were affected before we can claim that there is any geological significance in the disappearance of fossils of a particular type above a certain layer in the rocks. Secondly, there has recently been a fierce debate among evolutionists about the speed with which new species evolve. In some cases, an ancestral form can be identified in rocks spanning millions of years with little change, then, with no intermediate forms recorded, in the next layer of rocks there is a changed species, clearly descended from the parent form but with no intermediate steps visible. Does this mean that the change happened literally in one step, going from one generation to the next? Almost certainly not. The American evolutionary biologist Ledyard Stebbins provides a nice example of what may really be happening, in his book *Darwin to DNA*.

Stebbins imagines that evolution sets to work on an animal the size of a mouse, in such a way that larger animals are more successful – perhaps there is a climatic change which favours larger individuals, because they are better able to retain their body heat. Whatever the reason, suppose that selection acts to favour individuals that are a tiny bit larger than average, while individuals that are a tiny bit smaller than average are at a disadvantage. 'Tiny' really is the word that matters, because Stebbins sets the figure so small that it could not be detected in one generation by any human biologist today. It would take 12,000 generations for this hypothetical evolutionary pressure to produce animals the size of an elephant from ancestors the size of a mouse. By assuming that each generation takes five years to reach maturity (longer than the lifetime of a mouse, but less than that of an elephant) Stebbins concludes that an elephant-like animal can evolve from a mouse-like ancestor in 60,000 years, while at each step (each generation) the parents and offspring would be indistinguishable by any test we could apply. Mice may indeed be evolving into elephants, or the other way around, before our very eyes, without us noticing.

By human standards, evolution is a slow process. And yet, an interval of just 60,000 years is too *short* to be measured by geological techniques. The emergence of a 'new' life form in less than 100,000 years is, as far as the record in the rocks is concerned, 'instantaneous'. If there are fossil remains now being formed, in layers near the surface of the ground, they probably include the bones of many kinds of dog that have lived alongside human beings. Perhaps, in a hundred million years time, there will be paleontologists on Earth (visitors from other planets?) who study those remains. To them, it will seem as if the chihuahua appeared overnight, in going from one layer of rocks to the next. Although they will be able to identify the wolf as an ancestor of the chihuahua, such future paleontologists will have no hope of reconstructing all the small and subtle steps in the evolutionary processes that converted one animal into the other. Nevertheless, those tiny steps are really the way evolution works.

Important breaks in the geological record are the ones where many different kinds of individuals die. Sometimes, life on land is affected more than life in the oceans; sometimes it is the other way around. Sometimes animals suffer while plants survive relatively unscathed, and so on. One way of measuring the severity of an extinction of life forms is in terms of the way biologists classify living things. The main division is into five separate kingdoms, which include animals, plants, fungi and two types of single-celled life form. All known forms of life fall into one of these five categories. No ecological disaster on Earth has yet been severe enough to wipe out a whole kingdom. We can look at the subdivisions of the animal kingdom by following through the lines that we belong to – there are similar subdivisions in other kingdoms.

The next step down from a kingdom is the phylum. From our point of view, the important distinction among animal phyla is between the one for animals with backbones (chordates) and those for animals without backbones (invertebrates). There are five classes of chordates, the mammals (to which we belong), birds, amphibians, reptiles and fish. In the past, some extinction events *have* wiped out whole classes, both in the animal kingdom and in others. Such extinctions are rare, and show up clearly as important events in the geological record.

Within the mammal class, there are several orders, ours being the primates, each of which subdivides into families. The primate families are the hominids, the great apes, the gibbons, old world monkeys and new world monkeys. At the next level comes the genus, in our case *Homo*, and finally the species, *Homo sapiens*. In the standard classification, both of these last two subdivisions are occupied by ourselves in splendid isolation – an example of human chutzpah, or homo chauvinism, because by any objective standards (perhaps those of the hypothetical extraterrestrial paleontologist examining our fossil remains 100 million years from now) it would make more sense to group the two types of chimpanzee (and perhaps the gorilla as well) with *Homo* as one genus (or, if you prefer, to discard the genus Homo and classify ourselves as a variety of chimpanzee). But that is not an argument we want to get into here (it will already be familiar to readers of our earlier book). What matters now is that species (and genera) often disappear from the fossil record, but leave their cousins alive and well (chimps may very soon go this way, as the tropical rainforest is destroyed, but future fossil hunters will find plenty of bones of *Homo sapiens* from strata laid down long after the death of the chimps). The disappearance of a whole family, on the other hand, is more unusual, and if several families disappear at the same time that hints at widespread environmental changes, while the disappearance of whole classes of plants or animals, on land or in the sea, is an even clearer sign of a global catastrophe.

Over the 590 million years since the Precambrian, many families have evolved, gone through changes, and faded out, to be replaced by other forms of life. About half a dozen families of marine animals go extinct every million years or so, and such an extinction rate is therefore not unusual in the history of life on Earth. But there are four occasions, at about 438 Myr, 253 Myr, 213 Myr and 65 Myr, when many more families (as many at 15 to 20 in a million-year interval) were wiped out. These are the great extinctions which nobody disputes. In addition, there is a marginal case a little over 360 Myr ago, and many well-established lesser extinctions which affected species and genera but did not wipe out whole families. As you might expect, the four or five most dramatic extinctions each mark a turning point in the evolution of life. The geological record shows that they did indeed occur at times of environmental changes, and in particular it seems that many forms of life have been wiped from the face of the Earth each time our planet has suffered a major cooling and an ice age (or a series of ice ages). We are descended from species that have survived all these crises, and already in that sense we can regard ourselves as children of the ice, although there is a much closer connection between human origins and ice ages which we shall develop later. The first question that this discovery raises, which has to be answered before we can take the story of life any further, is *why* the environment should change so dramatically from time to time. Blame today is laid at the doors of two processes. One is slow but certain, and definitely played a part in shaping the environmental changes that have produced us; the other is swift and spectacular, cannot explain all the extinctions seen in the fossil record, but almost certainly provided a 'last straw' effect that brought a dramatic conclusion to the age of the dinosaurs and ushered in the age of the mammals.

Our changing planet

Continents move about the face of the globe. The geography of our planet is a changing feature of the environment. This discovery was one of the major scientific events of the past fifty years. Although speculation about the remarkable jigsaw-puzzle-like fit between the outlines of South America and Africa goes back at least to the time of Francis Bacon, and the idea of continental drift surfaced in respectable science through the work of Alfred Wegener in the second decade of the twentieth century, it was only in 1962 that Harry Hess, of Princeton University, put forward the key proposal in what became the modern version of continental drift, the theory of plate tectonics.

Before then, supporters of the idea had to argue that the major land masses of the world had reached their present positions by ploughing through the thinner crust of sea-floor that lines the ocean basins – rather like big icebergs crunching their way through a thin layer of pack ice. This 'mechanism' simply could not be made to work. The sea-floor crust may be thinner than the crust of material that makes up the continents, but it is still solid rock, and would not conveniently move out of the way as the continents ploughed past. But over the decades more and more evidence had accumulated to show that continents now separated by thousands of miles of ocean had indeed once been part of the same land mass. Fossils formed part of that evidence – similar remains in similar rock strata in many parts of the world. The alignments of the rock strata themselves, and the scars left by the grinding of ancient glaciers across the rocks, showed that, for example, southern South America, southern Africa, south Australia and India had once been locked together under a blanket of ice. The reason it took so long for continental drift to become respectable was that nobody had a satisfactory mechanism. So Hess's suggestion was welcomed with a sigh of relief in many quarters, and continental drift became respectable almost overnight.

The breakthrough came with the realization that instead of continents moving through the crust of the ocean floor, it is large 'plates' of mainly oceanic crust that are in motion, with continents simply carried along on their backs. In some places (notably down the middle of the Atlantic Ocean) there are great cracks in the sea-floor, underwater mountains and a seething maelstrom of volcanic activity. New oceanic crust is being forced up out of these cracks in the form of molten rock, which sets and is pushed out on either side, separating the continents further apart in the process. In other parts of the world (for example, along the western margin of the Pacific), thin oceanic crust is being pushed down underneath the edge of a thicker continent. As the crust is pushed down into the hotter layers of the Earth beneath, it melts; where it scrapes under the continent, mountains are forced upward, volcanoes belch forth, and earthquakes are common. The islands of Japan are a product of this kind of activity.

Long ago, South America and Africa *were* part of a single supercontinent, now called Pangea, which included almost all of the Earth's continental crust. They were cracked and split apart by the development of the active volcanic feature that is now a spreading ridge in the middle of what has become the Atlantic Ocean, which is still getting wider. There is no spreading ridge in the middle of the North Pacific, which is steadily shrinking as the American plate is pushed westward. if the process continues undisturbed, eventually the Pacific will shrink into nothing, and North America will collide with Asia.

This is only the briefest caricature of continental drift at work. The theory is now thoroughly well founded, based on an enormous amount of data from geology. The icing on the cake, to answer any remaining Doubting Thomases, came in the 1980s, when range-finding measurements using laser beams from different continents, bounced off artificial satellites orbiting the Earth, made surveying so precise that the drift of the continents could be measured. Europe and America really are moving further apart, at exactly the rate (a couple of centimetres a year) required by plate tectonics theory.

Reconstructing the past geography of the globe is a difficult and painstaking task, which gets harder the further back you look. But geologists are now up to the task, and we can use the pictures they provide without worrying too much about the details of how the reconstructions are made. There is no doubt that about 250 million years ago, late in the Permian Period, virtually all the continents were grouped into one landmass, Pangea, which covered the South Pole and stretched in an arc across one side of the Earth almost to the North Pole. Pangea broke up into two continents, Laurasia in the north and Gondwanaland in the south, and these (especially Gondwanaland) fragmented further as the pieces drifted into roughly the places we see them today.

Before Pangea formed, back around 550 Myr when life was not even beginning to move on to land, the world was a very different place. Continents were strung out across the equatorial region of the Earth, and the dominant landmass was an earlier version of Gondwanaland which included large areas of what are now Antarctica, Africa and South America. The poles were covered by ocean, and ice free. It would have been a warm and pleasant world to live in – except that the continents were all barren deserts, bare rock (and, perhaps, sand), without a trace of soil or life.

The main effect that continental drift has in changing the environment of the Earth, making it more or less suitable for life, is by altering the temperature of the globe. This happens in two principal ways. The direct interrelationship between geography and climate is not entirely straightforward, but cutting it down to essentials it depends on the ease with which warm water from the tropics can circulate to high latitudes. Tropical oceans are warmed strongly by the Sun, which is virtually overhead throughout the year; at high latitudes, the amount of solar heat that can be absorbed depends on the season, and very little of this heat is available in winter. But if warm ocean currents (like the Gulf Stream today) can penetrate to high latitudes, they can help to keep the high latitudes free from the grip of ice (which is why Ireland is a more pleasant place to live than Alaska). When there is a continent near the pole (or right over it, as is the case with Antarctica today), ocean currents cannot keep the region warm. The land provides a solid base on which snow can settle, building up into great ice sheets. And the shiny white surface of the ice sheets and snow fields reflects away even the summer heat of the Sun, keeping the polar region locked in the grip of ice and lowering the average temperature over the whole globe. By and large, this is bad for life.

The second way in which tectonic activity changes global temperatures is through its influence on volcanic activity. Sometimes there is a lot of tectonic activity, with continents being crushed together and new mountain ranges being thrown up. Sometimes there is less activity. All of the present day atmosphere of the Earth is a product of volcanic activity, gases spewed out over millions of years, in fits and starts. One effect of the atmosphere is that it acts like a blanket around the Earth, holding in warmth that would otherwise escape into space. The process is called the 'greenhouse effect', although in fact it works quite differently from the way in which a greenhouse holds in heat. The greenhouse effect is more effective, and the Earth is therefore warmer, when there is more carbon dioxide in the atmosphere (this is now a subject of environmental concern, because human activities, especially burning coal and oil, are increasing the amount of carbon dioxide around today). Carbon dioxide is one of the chief products of volcanic activity, but it is absorbed both by living things (as part of photosynthesis) and by the oceans, where it is dissolved and may be laid down as limestone rock. So the carbon dioxide concentration of the atmosphere has varied over geological time, as more or less of the gas has been poured out by volcanoes. We have no way, unfortunately, of measuring 'fossil' carbon dioxide from the atmosphere of millions of years ago, but when there is other geological evidence that the world was particularly warm we may suspect that this is a sign that the greenhouse effect was particularly strong at that time.

These two changes, linked with the changing geography of our planet, probably explain many of the climatic changes associated with the extinctions of life on Earth. But two other processes are also important enough to mention, before we get on to the meat of our story, the saga of life itself.

Bolts from Heaven

In recent years, the idea that mass extinctions may be caused by bolts from the skies has struck a chord in the popular imagination, and also with many scientists. The battered face of the Moon shows traces of the impact of many solid objects on its surface during its long lifetime. When space probes went into orbit around Mars and sent back detailed pictures of its surface, they showed similar cratering. Venus, hidden beneath a thick blanket of cloud, is more difficult to assess, but airborne photography, images from space and careful surveying of the surface of our own planet show that the Earth, too, bears the scars of a bombardment from space. Clearly, the inner part of the Solar System is a dangerous place to be; there are large objects around which collide with planets (and moons) from time to time.

Astronomers know what these objects are. A belt of rocky debris, the asteroids, orbits the Sun between the orbits of Mars and Jupiter. Some asteroids, lumps of rock up to several tens of kilometres across, dive across the Earth's orbit as they move around the Sun; and comets are frequent visitors to the inner part of the Solar System. An impact with any of these would leave a sizeable scar on the face of the Earth. Could such collisions create such a disturbance that they wipe many families of living things from the face of our planet?

The circumstantial evidence is impressive. Canada provides some particularly good examples, because much of the land surface of Canada is ancient rock with a long history, while because of the climate of Canada today ancient scars are not concealed by a lush covering of forest. At Minicouagan, for example, a ring-shaped feature 70 kilometres across is interpreted as the scar left by an impact 210 million years ago, when an asteroid more than a kilometre across struck the Earth. New Quebec Crater is a more recent feature, some five million years old, a circular lake three kilometres wide surrounded by a high mountain rim, looking exactly like a crater on the Moon. And these are small compared with some features, such as the circular Deep Bay, 13 kilometres in diameter, whose age has not been measured but which looks like the eroded remains of an ancient impact crater.

There is no doubt that our planet has been struck by bolts from Heaven in the past, and that it will be struck again. As recently as 1907 a great explosion occurred in the heart of Siberia, at Tunguska, devastating forests over an enormous area. Information about the blast only slowly leaked out from a wild and upopulated region of the globe, and investigations of the scene were later hampered by the turmoil of war and revolution in which Russia soon became embroiled. But the consensus among scientists today is that the event, equivalent to the explosion of several million tonnes of TNT, or a moderate sized nuclear weapon, was caused by a relatively small fragment of the icy core of a dead comet (essentially a cosmic iceberg) entering the Earth's atmosphere and either striking the ground or exploding near the ground as the heat raised by the friction of its passage through the atmosphere vaporized the ice. If the impact had taken place just a little further to the west, Moscow or Leningrad (then still St Petersburg) might have been destroyed, killing the men who were to lead the Russian revolution, and the history of the twentieth century might have been very different. And the Siberian explosion of 1907 didn't even leave a crater behind; it must have been modest indeed compared with some of the events that have scarred the Earth.

Very few paleontologists today would dispute the idea that such impacts have had an effect on life on Earth. Species, and perhaps genera, could quite easily have been wiped out in the aftermath of such disasters. But whole families? And not just one or two families, but a dozen or more? There are fierce arguments among the experts on just how big a role can be assigned to meteor and comet impacts as the causes of mass extinctions. The most widely publicized case concerns the death of the dinosaurs, 65 million years ago. Researchers from the University of California at Berkeley found, at the end of the 1970s, that layers of rock just this age, from several different parts of the world, contain a trace of iridium. Iridium, a heavy metal, is very rare on the surface of the Earth, although it is thought to occur in larger quantities deep inside our planet. It is much more common in the rocky remains of some kinds of meteorite. One explanation suggested for the iridium layer is that it was formed from the debris of a very large meteorite that struck the Earth just at the time the dinosaurs died out, at the end of the Cretaceous.

In this picture, the debris from the impact rose high into the air, forming a fine layer of dust, laced with iridium, in the upper atmosphere. The dust pall stretched around the world, blocking out the Sun. In the cold and dark beneath the dust pall, plants and animals died in profusion, and by the time the dust settled out of the atmosphere, forming an iridium-enhanced layer in sediments worldwide, the dinosaurs, among other species, had gone.

It is a chilling, evocative scenario (calculations of the so-called 'nuclear winter' that would be likely to follow a full-blooded nuclear exchange between the superpowers are, in fact, derived from calculations of this scenario for the death of the dinosaurs). But there are difficulties with it. First, and most crucially, the dinosaurs did not die out overnight, but over a period of millions of years. Different species disappear from the fossil record at slightly different times, suggesting that the catastrophe that struck them, though rapid by geological standards, was not as quick as the term 'death of the dinosaurs' seems to suggest. Secondly, iridium can also be provided in other ways. Most notably, it is one of the products of volcanic activity. The famous iridium layer may be telling us not that a giant meteor struck the Earth, but that there was an upwelling of volcanic activity at around this time. Volcanic activity can also chill the Earth, by pouring out dust into the stratosphere (or, indeed, it can warm the Earth, by pouring out carbon dioxide). It would be a more spread-out change in the environment than a meteor impact, lasting for hundreds of thousands, or millions, of years. And increased volcanic activity would be a result of changing tectonic conditions, alterations in the drift of continents about the globe.

One scenario, which ought to appeal to everybody but seems to offend proponents of both these ideas, regards meteorite impacts as a possible *cause* of volcanic activity. Large meteorites could punch holes right through the Earth's crust, especially where the crust is thin, under the oceans, allowing molten rock to flood out, and perhaps initiating a new phase of tectonic activity.

Holes in the sky

The debate continues, and is far from being settled. As if these were not enough hazards for life to contend with, the environment of our planet has changed drastically in other ways, as well. The Earth's magnetic field, for example, is not the fixed and constant guide that mariners would like it to be. Traces of magnetism in old rocks, frozen into the rocks when they were being laid down, show that from time to time the Earth's magnetic field reverses direction completely. Seven hundred thousand years ago, for example, the north *magnetic* pole was in Antarctica. A modern magnetic compass, carried back in time to that epoch, would point south, geographically speaking. In order to get where it is now, the north magnetic pole has swapped places with the south magnetic pole, which used to lie in the Arctic. In such a magnetic reversal, recorded by the fossil magnetism of successive layers of rock, the strength of the field first dies away to zero, and then builds up again, usually in the opposite direction, but sometimes in the same direction as before.

This discovery has caused some confusion among a certain kind of catastrophist. Some popular, but not very scientific, books refer to the Earth toppling over in space as the poles swap positions, or to the crust of the Earth slipping around so that the geographic poles change places. This is *not* what the record of fossil magnetism tells us. It is the dynamo deep inside the Earth, a swirling layer of electrically charged fluid, that changes, presumably because the flow of molten material around the core alters. The geography of the globe stays the same during a magnetic reversal – and indeed, we may be experiencing the beginning of such a reversal now, since the Earth's magnetic field is weaker, judging from the record in the rocks, than it was a few thousand years ago. The whole reversal typically takes several thousand years; once the field is established in a certain orientation, it may stay that way for as long as tens of millions of years, or for as little as a hundred thousand years.

Even though the geography of the globe does not change during a reversal, such an event could still be bad news for life on Earth. Our planet is constantly being bombarded by tiny charged particles from space, called cosmic rays. Most of the time, while the magnetic field is strong, these particles are held magnetically in the regions known as the Van Allen belts, hundreds of miles above the equator. Only a small proportion spill over and are deflected towards the polar regions, funnelling along the magnetic lines of force. There, their major contribution to the environment is to produce the spectacular displays of coloured lights in the sky that we call the auroras. But cosmic radiation of this kind could be quite hazardous to life, if there were no magnetic shield to protect us. The radiation is akin to some kinds of radiation produced by nuclear reactors, or bombs, and just as lethal, in large enough doses. One of the major medical concerns about the possibility of sending people to Mars, for example, is the worry about how astronauts' bodies might be affected by cosmic rays, especially if the Sun were to produce a large outburst during the several months it would take for a spacecraft to make the journey.

Magnetic reversals are probably not a good thing for life on the surface of the Earth (life in the seas, of course, has better protection from cosmic rays). It happens that reversals have been unusually common during the past 85 million years, with the field switching direction nearly 200 times. There was a similar burst of geomagnetic activity in the early Devonian, at about 400 Myr, but in between these active intervals reversals were decidedly rare. There was a short burst of magnetic reversal activity near the end of the Cretaceous, with five flips in the span of a million years; *perhaps* this had something to do with the death of the dinosaurs, though if so, it is surprising that nothing so dramatic occurs in the fossil record around 42 Myr, when there were 17 magnetic reversals in the space of three million years. Nevertheless, there is some tendency for intervals when the Earth's magnetic field is suffering several slips of this kind to 'coincide' with intervals when an unusually large number of species go extinct. There is also some evidence that magnetic reversals have been more common at the times when the Earth has suffered impacts from space. Naturally, this has led some scientists to speculate that the impacts *cause* the magnetic reversals, and that it is a combination of two disasters which then has an adverse effect on life.

This makes a lot of sense. A major impact could very well be just the thing to shake up the currents flowing in the Earth's core, and make them swirl about erratically. It could take a million years or more for the swirling currents to settle down, and this would stretch out the period of environmental disturbances caused by an initial short-lived event, the meteorite impact. But it will be very hard to prove this appealing scenario.

Looking further afield, there are other ways in which cosmic events can affect life on Earth. When a star explodes as a supernova, it sends cosmic rays sleeting across space. If a nearby star exploded in this way, then the Earth's magnetic field would provide inadequate protection from the cosmic storm, and many families on land would certainly die. It would be almost as bad if our Sun, which is prone to more modest outbursts, described as storms and flares, were to become slightly more active than it is today, just at a time when the Earth's magnetic shield was weakened during a reversal. Both of these possibilities have been raised by astronomers as explanations of the terminal Cretaceous event. In yet another variation on the theme, some people point out that a sudden flood of cosmic rays (caused by a supernova, or by a weakening of the magnetic shield) could disrupt the ozone layer, in the stratosphere, which shields us from harmful ultraviolet radiation from the Sun. The importance of the ozone layer to life on Earth is familiar to everyone who has followed the saga of chlorofluorocarbons (CFCs), the gases (used in spray cans, refrigerators, and in blowing the bubbles in foamed plastic) that are implicated in the appearance of holes in the ozone layer over Antarctica and the Arctic. Perhaps the dinosaurs died of sunburn and skin cancer.

But all such ideas suffer from the same flaw – they are special pleading, 'one off' explanations of an event that may be uniquely interesting to us, but which is far from being unique in the long history of our planet. Recently, there have been entertaining attempts to fit this event into a supposed cycle of extinctions.

Cycles of death

Species, genera and families are always going extinct – four or five families disappear every million years or so, throughout the fossil record. But when the numbers of genera going extinct in each million-year interval are plotted out on a time chart, intervals with higher than average extinction rates stand out. It is always tempting, when confronted with a wiggly line representing some natural, changing phenomenon, to see if there is any regular pattern in the wiggles. Several people have succumbed to this temptation in looking at the pattern of extinctions. Depending on just which peaks in the curve you choose to regard as particularly significant, and on exactly which timescale you adhere to (remember that there is some uncertainty in geological dates) there is some evidence for peak extinctions at this level to recur in waves, at intervals of something between 26 and 32 million years.

This may be a complete coincidence. A rather nice statistical argument suggests that the *appearance* of a 26-million-year periodicity should occur at random in the geological record. The argument goes like this. In a system which changes by the same amount at more or less regular intervals, at each change there is a 50:50 chance that the system will step up (more extinctions) or down (fewer extinctions). In that kind of sequence, known as a random walk, the most likely interval between *high* peaks is four steps. You can test this, if you are so inclined, with a piece of graph paper, a pencil and a coin. Starting out from the middle of the left-hand side of the paper, toss the coin and draw a line which goes one square to the right and either one square up the page or one square down the page depending on whether you toss a head or a tail. Keep going across the page, and you should end up with a series of wiggles about four squares apart.

What has this to do with extinction cycles? Simply that the average geological age lasts for a little over six million years. *Small* extinctions, nothing to do with cosmic catastrophes, are spaced about that far apart. So, using random walk statistics, unusually high extinction rates ought to occur at roughly 26-million-year intervals (four times six-and-a-bit). The actual geological record, over the past 140 million years, shows two good peaks that fit the 26-million-year cycle, two less impressive peaks in the right places, and two gaps – much more like random variations than a precise cycle.

This is a shame in a way, since the astronomers had two beautiful ideas to explain a perfect periodicity in the range from 26 to 32 million years. Both depend on the fact that comets originate in a large cloud of material, which forms a spherical shell around the sun, far beyond the orbit of Pluto. The ones we see are simply stragglers from this cloud, disturbed and sent shooting in past the Sun by some chance encounter with a neighbour. If there was a way to make a big disturbance in the comet cloud, it might rain comets in the inner Solar System for hundreds of thousands of years, with many of the objects colliding with the Earth in a burst of destruction far greater than that caused by the impact of a single meteorite. But how do you disturb the comet cloud?

This is where astronomical ingenuity comes in. According to one theory, the cloud is repeatedly, and regularly, disturbed as the Sun and its family of planets bob up and down (like the needle of a sewing machine passing through a sheet of material) through the star systems that form the plane of our Milky Way Galaxy, a great disc-shaped system of stars, dust and gas. According to the second theory, the disturbing influence lies much closer to home – either a dark star, in orbit around our Sun and passing through the cloud every 26 million years or so (the so-called 'death star' or 'Nemesis'), or an undiscovered planet, orbiting beyond Pluto and exerting its gravitational influence on the comets ('Planet X'). Think of a star so far from the Sun that it takes 26 million years to orbit

around once (a 'year' 26 million years long), and you begin
to have some idea of how good astronomers are at imagining
things.

It would be much easier to accept all this as more than
science fictional speculation if there were six clear peaks in the
extinction record of the past 140 million years, spaced at
precise 26-million-year intervals. As you may have guessed, we
don't believe it for a minute. But the story of Nemesis and
Planet X is important, even if it is science fiction, because it
demonstrates how easy it is to think of ways to cause
widespread death and destruction among the life forms that
inhabit the Earth.

Death is a way of life

From a broad perspective, the death of the dinosaurs at the
end of the Cretaceous, and other extinctions which have
occurred both before and since, were not so remarkable.
Conditions on Earth do change over a long period of time,
largely as a result of continental drift. When they change
drastically enough, there are extinctions which show up in the
fossil record. The late Cretaceous, for example, was a time
when the world cooled through these long term processes, and
there was a gradual decline in the number of dinosaur (and
other) species over millions of years. Perhaps some bolt from
the skies did then provided a last-straw effect, ushering in, as
we shall see, the age of the mammals.

It is fun to speculate about disaster from above, and to
wonder how life can continue at all on Earth, subject to the
hazards of cosmic collisions, magnetic reversals, holes in the
sky, supernova explosions, dark stars and so on. Frankly,
though, we do not really care – at least from the point of view
of the present book – whether any or all of these contributed
to the changes at the end of the Cretaceous. It is a fact
that the environment changed at that time, and that those
environmental (especially climatic) changes had a profound
influence on the evolution of life. Without them, we would
not be here. *Whatever* the ultimate cause of those environmental
changes, it is the way the changing environment changed the
pattern of life that interests us here and now. In later chapters,

we will look in more detail at more recent environmental changes; there, we can talk with much more certainty about why the climate changed. But even so, what really matters to us now is not the cause of those changes, but the way in which those climatic changes, whatever their cause, were directly responsible for our own existence, and yours.

In telling that tale, we do not *need* to invoke cosmic catastrophes to explain the broad sweep of environmental changes which are so clearly related to the rise and fall of different forms of life on Earth. Almost always in science, it turns out that the simplest solution to a puzzle is the best, and the simplest explanation of the major extinctions in the fossil record is that they have been brought about by the long, slow processes of continental drift and the resulting environmental changes, especially ice ages. The changing environment has a strong influence on which species (and families) survive and which ones fall by the evolutionary wayside; death is a way of life, in the changing environment of planet Earth. But life itself, in one form or another, is very persistent. The story of how our ancestors survived, through long intervals of geological time and changing environmental conditions, to become the heirs to the dinosaurs, highlights the tenaciousness of a family even under adverse conditions.

2

The Heir to the Dinosaurs

Our ancestors were the ancestors of the dinosaurs. We – the mammals – inherited the Earth when the dinosaur line died out. It is rather as if a wealthy woman with no children left her estate to the children of her cousin, who shared the same grandparents, but had no closer relationship to the benefactor. The analogy is not perfect, because the dinosaurs did not 'die out' in the sense that no dinosaur left any descendants behind. True, many lines did 'go extinct', but others evolved and adapted to changing circumstances. Birds are descended from dinosaurs, and according to some classifications birds *are* dinosaurs. But birds do not dominate the Earth today. They achieve their success by occupying specialist niches where they are not in direct competition with mammals – an ironic turn-round from the day of the dinosaur, when mammals survived by occupying specialist niches that were not in direct competition with the dominant dinosaurs. Who knows – maybe in a hundred million years from now, descendants of birds will dominate the Earth and the age of the mammals will seem like a temporary aberration in evolution. Judging from the record of the past few hundred million years, it wouldn't be all that surprising.

Crises in the sea

One of the clearest examples of the effects of continental drift on life on Earth occurs in the fossil record from a time before life emerged on to the land. At the end of the Ordovician Period, around 438 million years ago, there were massive extinctions; this may have been, in terms of the proportion of species affected, the second-greatest catastrophe to strike during the history of life on Earth to date. Geologists are able to reconstruct maps of the supercontinent of Gondwanaland as it was at that time, and they have shown that areas of land that are now South America, Africa (including Arabia), India, Antarctica and Australia formed one continent in the late Ordovician, and that this continent drifted over the South Pole at that time. These are just the geographical conditions that ought to encourage the spread of ice. Warm water is cut off from the polar regions; land lies ready to form a base on which snow can accumulate and build up into ice sheets; ice sheets, once formed, reflect away incoming solar heat and chill the globe still further.

This is exactly borne out by the geological record. Africa bears the scars of glaciation from the time when it lay over the pole, and the fossils from sediments being laid down at different latitudes also show signs of the cooling. As Gondwanaland moved to cover the pole, species that were adapted to cold-water conditions moved towards the equator, while species that had previously been found in the tropics died out altogether. Cold, spreading outward from the polar regions, explains the mass extinctions at the end of the Ordovician.

The events of 438 million years ago certainly provide a neat punctuation mark in our story, since it was during the periods that followed, the Silurian and the Devonian, that life began to move on to the land. Gondwanaland drifted slightly away from the South Pole once more, while pieces of land that now form parts of Britain and Europe, North America and Asia were scattered more or less around the equator, and the North Pole was covered by ocean. These scattered pieces of land were edged by extensive shallow seas, where plant life thrived in tidal waters. And it was warm – very probably, in large measure because of tectonic activity which spread carbon dioxide around the globe from volcanoes.

Carbon dioxide helps to warm the world, through the greenhouse effect. It is also the basic 'food' plants need, for photosynthesis. A blade of grass, or the trunk of a mighty oak, are both made chiefly of carbon, extracted from carbon dioxide in the air. It is hardly surprising that some of those plants in the tidal waters of the shallow seas of the Silurian gradually evolved and adapted to drier conditions, with their descendants eventually spreading on to the land. As the first land plants clustered around the river deltas and tidal flats, natural selection would favour any variation which gave a plant the ability to survive in slightly drier conditions, away from the crowd, where it could get unobstructed sunlight – another vital ingredient in photosynthesis.

Animal life followed plant life on to the land for the same reason – because of competition for both physical space and space in the ecology. Segmented sea-dwellers, ancestors of creatures such as millipedes, made the transition easily and early; cockroaches had evolved and were established well over 300 million years ago. Amphibian forms developed from fish, and moved on to the land to eat the plants and insects, not in some natural ascent up the glorious ladder of evolution, but because they found life too tough in the seas. *Successful* sea-dwellers, superbly adapted to their way of life, stayed in the seas. On the margins, less successful life forms found that they could eke out an existence by exploiting the newly available resources in the wet lands near the sea; they had to learn new tricks in order to survive at all.

Vertebrates, our direct ancestors, first moved on to the land at the end of the Devonian Period, about 360 million years ago. This was just *after* another great catastrophe, which had struck life in the seas around seven million years previously. This may be a coincidence. Or it may be that the late Devonian 'event' stirred the evolutionary pot and led directly to the emergence of vertebrates from the water.

Towards the end of the Devonian, Gondwanaland once again drifted across the South Pole. In the late Ordovician, the glaciers had grown over Africa, because Africa was directly over the pole; this time South America suffered first, because the part of Gondwanaland that is now South America lay directly over the pole. Geologists see clear evidence of two phases of glaciation, centred in different parts of Gondwanaland at different times. As for the fossils, in rocks from this geological time, some strata show evidence of a catastrophe that lasted for millions of years, with tropical life forms suffering most. This seems paradoxical, but is always the case during ice ages. If the whole world cools, from the poles to the equator, then life forms that are adapted to high latitude conditions can migrate towards the tropics, where the water used to be too warm for them. But life forms that are adapted to tropical conditions have nowhere left to go – there is nowhere for them that used to be warmer than the tropics and has now cooled to be just right for their needs. At least in part, the late Devonian extinctions seem to have been a re-run of the crisis at the end of the Ordovician.

But the plants that were now well established on land do not seem to have suffered greatly at this time. Some of the hardest-hit communities were the inhabitants of shallow seas and estuaries; and the change in fossil remains in some strata occurs so quickly, over a narrow layer corresponding to a very short geological interval, that some paleontologists, notably Digby McLaren, of the Geological Survey of Canada, think that there was an instantaneous, world-wide catastrophe. That bears the hallmarks of the impact of a cosmic object with the Earth. A giant meteorite striking the sea would create tsunamis that could devastate the communities of the shallow seas, and vaporize so much water that great swathes of cloud would form, shielding the Sun and cooling the world below.

We know for certain, from the geological evidence, that Gondwanaland moved over the pole and glaciers grew at the time of the late Devonian extinction; there is circumstantial evidence that the disaster was made worse by an impact event. But whatever the exact causes, what matters is that, once again, the Earth cooled and many forms of life went extinct as a result. After the Devonian, the evolutionary action moved on to the land, and amphibians appeared. Whether or not the late Devonian extinctions gave the amphibians a push, it provides another neat marker in the story.

Megadynasties and proto-mammals

The Devonian was followed by the Carboniferous, a period that gets its name because it was a time when great forests spread across swampy, low-lying land – trees that became preserved in the swampy sediments, compressed by geological forces and turned (eventually) into coal. Some of the coal that we burn in fireplaces, furnaces and factories today is the fossilized remains of trees that lived more than 300 million years ago. The Carboniferous Period lasted from 360 Myr to 286 Myr; modern geologists often divide the period into two, the Mississippian (from 360 Myr to 320 Myr) and the Pennsylvanian (from 320 Myr to 286 Myr), named after coal deposits of those ages found in two of the present-day states of the USA. The coal that is locked up in these deposits (and others around the world) used to be living trees, and the carbon that made those living trees and later became coal was taken out of the air, by those trees, in the form of carbon dioxide.

The carbon dioxide came from volcanoes, as it does today. It is not the case that there is a fixed amount of carbon dioxide in the air, which has to be shared out among all the living things that need it. On a geological timescale, the amount of carbon dioxide available varies. The balance between carbon dioxide production, as a result of tectonic activity, and the rate at which it is removed from the air by biological processes (in the sea as well as in the land) is one of the imponderables of Earth history. We can guess that the events of the Carboniferous, which led to huge quantities of carbon dioxide being taken out of the air and the carbon being locked away in the rocks, may have made the world cooler than it might otherwise have been, since the greenhouse effect would have been weakened. But since we do not know how much carbon dioxide was produced by volcanoes at the time, we have no way to assess the 'might have been' in the equation. 'Cooler' the globe probably was, as a result of all the coal making. But cooler than what? We shall never know; but even though our main interest is in the evolution of animal life on land in the 300-odd million years that followed the Carboniferous, the existence of those coal deposits – and others – may yet have a part to play in our story.

The tale of animal life in that 300-million-year interval can be summarized in terms of four major developments, what Robert Bakker, of the University of Colorado, in Boulder, has called the 'Megadynasties'. Bakker took paleontology by the scruff of its neck and gave it a vigorous shake in the 1970s. He overturned long-held views on the nature of dinosaurs and their ancestors, and established beyond reasonable doubt that many dinosaurs were hot-blooded, active creatures. His once-revolutionary ideas are now respectable, although the image of the slow, lumbering dinosaur, with a brain the size of a pea, persists in many introductions to Earth history. Bakker's book, *The Dinosaur Heresies*, is required reading for anyone curious about the way life has evolved; here, we follow his lead in describing the four Megadynasties.

During the Carboniferous, and the early part of the Permian Period that followed, the first Megadynasty emerged. Amphibians came first. Like fish, they were cold-blooded; and although they could breathe air and live and feed out of water, they had to return to the water to reproduce, in a life cycle very similar to that of the modern frog, or the salamander. This didn't stop them reaching respectable sizes – several metres long, with bodies basically resembling that of the alligator, with squat legs jutting sideways from their bodies, and bellies close to the ground. About the end of the Carboniferous, a major evolutionary development occurred, but still within Bakker's first Megadynasty. Some species developed the hard-shelled egg. This freed it from the need to reproduce in water. The eggs, with their protective cover, could be laid in a nest on land, and the young could develop in a moist world of their own, inside the egg, until they had reached a stage where they could cope with life in the dry conditions outside, and would emerge from the shell. The egg layers are called reptiles – although there are other distinctions between amphibians and reptiles, this is the one that really matters.

These first reptiles, however, were still members of Mega-dynasty I. They were cold-blooded lumberers – in fact rather like the old image of dinosaurs. Bakker tells how measurements of the spacing between preserved fossil footprints show that these early reptiles were slow walkers, while studies of fossil bones show that the musculature attached to those bones could have made the fastest gait of the greatest predator of the time, *Dimetrodon*, no more than 'a lumbering waddle'. Until halfway through the Permian, the picture stayed much the same. The fossil record shows that there was little diversification of these animals, with just one big family of herbivores and just one big family of predators. This fits the picture of slow-moving creatures with low metabolic rates in a stable world, spreading over the land that had so recently, in terms of geological time, been colonized by plants.

Everything changed, however, halfway through the Permian Period, perhaps 270 million years ago, at the time of the Kazanian epoch. Bakker calls this 'the Kazanian Revolution', a time when 'the entire somnolent world of Megadynasty I passed away' (p. 409). The reason for the revolution, he argues, is that during the Kazanian some species became warm-blooded. Proto-mammals had arrived on the scene, and with a higher metabolic rate, including the ability to run fast, they swept their somnolent predecessors from the evolutionary stage.

There is no doubt that things changed dramatically at that time. Where there had been one family of predators, soon there were four; where there had been one family of plant eaters, there were five. Species proliferated, adapting to fill every ecological niche available, and evolution moved faster as a result of competition between species. Measurements of fossil remains confirm that these fast-evolving species were active and must have been warm-blooded. The structure of their bones, and the nature of their joints, show that the limbs of these creatures were driven by powerful muscles capable of giving them a good turn of speed, while the position of those limbs, straighter and more centrally under the body than those of earlier species, also shows adaptation to a more 'modern' form of locomotion.

Geography also enters into the argument. Animals that live on land are more sensitive to relatively small and short-lived changes in temperature than life in the sea. The ocean acts as a buffer, taking a long time to warm up, and a long time to cool down, when conditions change. This, of course, is why an island like Britain, on the edge of the ocean, never experiences either the baking heat of summer or the bitter cold of winter that occurs in a continental interior, in a place like Siberia. In the Kazanian, and throughout the late Permian, all the main land masses of the globe were joined in the supercontinent of Pangea. Gondwanaland was still near the South Pole, but joined to land which stretched continuously up across the equator and almost to the North Pole, with what is now Siberia, as it happens, at the highest northern latitudes. This must have made the world cool, even when there was not a full ice age, and warm-blooded animals would have an advantage over their cold-blooded cousins in cool conditions. Cold-blooded animals rely on the warmth of the Sun to stir them into life, and enable the biochemical processes that make their muscles work to become effective. Warm-blooded creatures, however, derive their heat from inside, using the energy from the food they eat, and can stay active and mobile when cold-blooded creatures are sluggish. (Even if the first warm-blooded creatures only gained a little warmth in this way, that would still give them a huge advantage over animals that were totally dependent on external warmth.)

The proto-mammals were hit by at least two important extinctions during the remainder of the Permian, and each time the survivors recovered and new species evolved to fill the ecological niches left vacant. Almost certainly, these extinctions were related to the unusual geography of the globe at that time, which must have made it easy for waves of cold to sweep over the land, even if the seas were not severely affected by a short-lived dip in climate. Just possibly, one or both of the extinctions was caused by a meteor impact. But Megadynasty II seemed to have proved its adaptability and warm-blooded worth over an interval of more than 20 million years, and to be all set for continued world domination, when the greatest disaster in the geological record struck the Earth. We can best put this, and subsequent events, in a proper perspective by backtracking a little to look at the nature of the proto-mammals whose promising evolutionary careers were so abruptly cut short, and whose descendants found, in the Triassic Period, that they had hazards other than the weather to cope with.

Mammals with a lisp

The warm-blooded, semi-reptilian proto-mammals that lived in the Permian, and some of which survived into the Triassic, were the direct ancestors of every mammal that has ever lived. You and us, cats and dogs, bats, whales, mongooses and giraffes, are all descended from therapsids, an order that seems to have been named by a paleontologist with a lisp. It is a sign of the difficulty of assigning extinct species to the standard classification of life that this order is officially part of the reptile class, although in the living world mammals, which are descended from the Therapsida, are a separate class ranked alongside reptiles. But we'll let that pass. Half-and-half creatures have to go in one category or the other, and since true mammals hadn't evolved then, that only leaves one class for the therapsids to go in.

How, though, do you distinguish between a mammal and a reptile (or between a proto-mammal and a reptile) – especially when you are dealing, not with living individuals in front of you, but with scraps of fossilized bone from rock strata hundreds of millions of years old? Most of us can list a few differences between mammals and reptiles off the top of our heads. But be careful. Probably one of the first things that springs to mind is that reptiles (such as snakes) are cold-blooded. But Bakker has taught us that many reptiles may have been hot-blooded in the past (and since birds, which are hot-blooded, are descended from dinosaurs, which were descended from reptiles, there is some living evidence that he is right). Better leave that one off the list. So, what characteristics should we concentrate on? Mammals are covered in hair, while reptiles are scaly – but hair and skin don't leave much trace in the fossil record. Reptiles lay eggs, while mammals bring forth their young alive, and suckle them; but the relevant bits of biological apparatus do not fossilize, either. To the paleontologist, bones are the only clues to work with, and there are several skeletal differences that make it possible to classify individuals as more or less mammalian. What they often come down to, surprising as it may seem, is the structure of the small bones in the ear.

Reptiles have a middle ear which contains one bone, used to transmit sound vibrations inward. Mammals, including ourselves, have ears that contain three bones (hammer, anvil and stirrup), which provide a more sensitive listening mechanism that works over a broader range of sound frequencies. In all probability, reptiles are literally incapable of appreciating Bach.

Fossil remains show that this structure developed over a long period of evolutionary time, and that the two 'extra' bones in the mammal ear (hammer and anvil) are adapted from bones that are part of the jaw structure in reptiles. We hear and appreciate Bach with the aid of bones that reptiles use when chewing. Among other things, the nature of the ear bones revealed from studies of fossil skulls enables paleontologists to tell whether an individual from the Permian or Triassic was more like a mammal or more like a reptile (they also, incidentally, provide a beautiful example of Darwinian evolution at work, and give the lie to ill-informed 'creationists' who claim that there is no evidence for the step-by-step evolution of complex parts of the body such as ears).

In fact, it is not so much true to say that mammals evolved 'from' reptiles, but rather that both evolved from amphibians. In the late Carboniferous, there was a variety of reptile forms around, but only two of these were to play a major part in the subsequent story of life on Earth. One group, the diapsids, kept what we regard as typical reptilian characteristics, and their line led to modern lizards, crocodiles and birds, as well as to the now extinct dinosaurs and flying reptiles. The other group, the synapsids, did much better than the diapsids at first, but their descendants suffered an almost terminal setback in the Triassic, before seizing their opportunity, as mammals, when the dinosaurs disappeared.

Synapsids came in two main varieties – two orders. First, there were the pelycosaurs, which appeared in late Carboniferous time, almost 300 million years ago, and had died out by the end of the Permian, some 50 million years later. They were members of Bakker's Megadynasty I, cold-blooded, lizard-like creatures with a sluggish lifestyle. These gave way to the therapsids in an explosion of evolutionary development following the 'invention' of internal warming mechanisms in the middle Permian. The therapsids came in so many varieties that we cannot even list them here. The range included: creatures rather like heavy-set dogs, that probably browsed among vegetation in and around shallow water; large, cow-like forms whose remains are found in early Triassic rocks from South America, South Africa and Russia; bear-like carnivores a couple of metres long; and a species known as Moschops which had a very thick skull, and probably went in for head-bashing contests, rather in the way goats do today.

By the early triassic, almost 250 million years ago, the carnivorous *Cynognathus* was around. Individuals of this species were about as big as a modern badger, with a big head and a short tail; they were almost certainly covered in fur rather than a scaly skin, as was *Thrinaxodon*, a smaller, stoat-sized creature from the same geological period. The therapsid that most closely resembled a mammal, however, occurred slightly later, and its remains are found in rocks from the early Jurassic, around 200 million years ago. This was *Probainognathus*, a member of the sub-order of therapsids known as the Cynodonts. It had a skull, jaw and teeth very like those of mammals, and like *Cynognathus* and *Thrinaxodon* members of *Probainognathus* were probably furry creatures – they may even have suckled their young. But they were much smaller than their two predecessors, and played only a minor role in the story of life during the Jurassic. Their descendants evolved into three kinds of early mammals, one of which went extinct, one of which was the forerunner of modern egg-laying mammals (such as the duck-billed platypus), and one of which, *Kuehneotherid*, was the ancestor of every other mammal alive on Earth today. Such an important future role for *Kuehneotherid's* descendants would have been scarcely credible, however, for any alien zoologist visiting Earth during the 183 million years from the beginning of the Triassic to the end of the Cretaceous. Large therapsids had been swept away, first by some natural catastrophe and then by competition of the superior life forms that evolved from the other reptilian line, the diapsids, and became the dinosaurs. Bakker's Megadynasty III dominated the scene. Two hundred million years ago, you wouldn't have bet good money that the *Probainognathus* line would one day inherit the Earth.

The day of the dinosaur

The wave of extinctions that struck at the end of the Permian was the greatest in the fossil record. It was not just the end of a period of geological time, but literally the end of an era, the Paleozoic. The Mesozoic Era, which includes three periods (Triassic, Jurassic and Cretaceous) began with a bang, 248 million years ago. Just as the amphibians were washed ashore in the aftermath of late Devonian extinctions, so the day of the dinosaur was preceded, and probably triggered, by the extinctions at the end of the Permian.

In the seas, the terminal Permian extinctions wiped out between 75 and 90 per cent of all existing species. They took place over an interval of about ten million years, just at the time when Pangea was assembling almost all of the land surface of the Earth in one mass stretching from the South Pole to the North. Just as in the cases of the extinctions at the end of the Ordovician and the Devonian, a variety of geological evidence reveals that the Earth cooled in the late Permian, and the primary reason for this cooling was undoubtedly the way the changing geography of the globe altered the circulation patterns of warm ocean currents and allowed ice to spread over at least one of the polar regions. Because the Permian catastrophe was so severe, it is tempting to speculate that cosmic collisions may also have played a part. But whatever caused the cooling, the cooling had a dramatic impact on life on land, as well as on life in the sea. This was the first great extinction of land-based life. After the end of the Permian, the world looked like a different planet, as the surviving life forms diversified and adapted to the changed conditions.

At first, the therapsids seemed to recover well from the catastrophe, just as their ancestors had recovered from lesser extinctions during the second half of the Permian. Large animals had been wiped out in the disaster, while smaller creatures survived. This is a typical pattern in extinctions of land-based fauna, and can be explained naturally if the disaster killed off large amounts of vegetation. Large herbivores would starve as their food supply withered away (even if they could survive the cold) and large carnivores would starve if there were no large herbivores to feed on. Smaller creatures which needed less food (and which could find shelter from the harsh weather conditions) would have a better chance of survival. In the space of a few million years, the small proto-mammalian survivors of the terminal Permian catastrophe had evolved new lines of large grazers and carnivores. But at the same time, the other variety of reptiles, the diapsids, were evolving and adapting to the changing conditions.

While conditions were relatively stable, before the end of the Permian, the ecological niches for large animals were filled by proto-mammals, and no new lines could get a look in. When those large species were wiped out, both the small therapsids and the more reptilian small diapsids had an opportunity to diversify. The result was a genuine clash between two different variations on the evolutionary theme, starting out on an equal footing. It is a sobering reminder to us as mammals that there is nothing intrinsically superior about the mammal way of life (that we are not 'higher up' some hypothetical evolutionary ladder), to learn that our ancestors lost this equal battle.

Their reptilian rivals of the early Triassic were the thecodonts, small animals about as big as a modern dog. Like the proto-mammals, they had limbs placed underneath their bodies, well able to support their weight and give them a good turn of speed. Some of them could run on two legs, balancing with the aid of a long tail held out behind them. They must have been warm-blooded, in order to compete so successfully with therapsids (quite apart from other evidence of a high metabolic rate, which Bakker has collated), and as the line became increasingly successful individual members of some species reached a weight of half a ton. In an explosion of evolutionary success and diversification, thecodonts were soon replaced by the archosaurs – forerunners of the dinosaurs, the crocodiles and the flying reptiles (the pterosaurs).

Bakker has described how in the early Triassic the herbivore community was dominated by members of the therapsid order, known as cynodonts. These were preyed upon by other varieties of cynodont and, at first, just a few species of archosaur. Over the next 35 million years, up to the end of the Triassic, the pattern, revealed by the numbers of fossils of different species found in rock strata, gradually changed. First, the number of predator cynodonts declined, while the number of predator archosaurs increased. Up to the middle of the Triassic, the herbivorous cynodonts were still doing quite well, although after 230 Myr they were being eaten not by their close relatives in the therapsid order but by their more distant archosaur cousins. At about this time, at least one branch of archosauria became the dinosaurs, and the dinosaurs rapidly evolved both new varieties of carnivore and varieties of grazer. Not only were the remaining cynodonts being eaten by dinosaurs, their food was being eaten by other dinosaurs, who must have been more efficient grazers than our closer relations, since by the early Jurassic, a little over 200 million years ago, cynodonts had all but disappeared from the scene. The survivors, the line from *Kuehneotherid* to *Probainognathus* to ourselves, made it by evolving into small, mouse-like creatures, too insignificant for dinosaurs to take much notice of, leading a probably nocturnal lifestyle and living off insects and, perhaps, plants. The day of the dinosaur had arrived.

If you want to know more about dinosaurs, you will have to get hold of Bakker's book, and the one by John Noble Wilford, both mentioned in our bibliography. From the end of the Triassic, 213 million years ago, to the end of the Cretaceous, nearly 150 million years later, dinosaurs ruled the world. This is over twice as long as the time that has elapsed since the 'death of the dinosaurs'; our own line has been distinct from the lines leading to other African apes for no more than five million years, less than 4 per cent of the 'day' of the dinosaur. (If the domination of the dinosaurs had lasted for 24 hours, then the equivalent lifetime of our line so far is about 12 minutes short of an hour.)

While dinosaurs roamed the Earth, Pangea broke apart, first into Laurasia and Gondwanaland, then into separate fragments which drifted around the globe and began to group together in new patterns. Flowering plants, although they had appeared in an early form in the Triassic, burst out into something like their modern forms halfway through the day of the dinosaur, in the mid-Cretaceous. Bakker argues that dinosaurs were directly responsible for the evolution of flowers, because their voracious munching of vegetation gave an evolutionary edge to plants that evolved better means of reproduction, with a dinosaur being, to a plant, part of the mechanism of natural selection (grasses, however, did not appear until after the dinosaurs had already left the evolutionary stage). And at least four important extinctions struck life on Earth while dinosaurs dominated the scene. All of this, however, lies outside the scope of the present book. Just two factors are relevant to us now. What might have become of the dinosaurs, if the world had not changed 65 million years ago? And what was it that wiped them from the face of the Earth?

Heirs to the dinosaurs?

In fact, 'dinosaurs' never existed – at least, not in the official scientific classification of animals. The term was invented by the British paleonotologist Richard Owen in 1841, to describe what he regarded as 'a distinct tribe' of reptiles identifiable from their fossil bones (Bakker, *The Dinosaur Heresies*, p. 20). The name comes from two Greek words, *deinos* and *sauros*, together meaning 'terrible lizard'; the popular image of dinosaurs certainly fits the name, although there were also placid, cow-like browsers that have to go by the name dinosaur if any ancient reptiles deserve the name. Although Owen's suggestion caught the popular imagination, however, it never became part of the scientific classification. 'Dinosaur' is a name which actually covers two distinct orders of reptile, the Saurischia and the Ornithischia. These names derive from features of their anatomy, saurischians with more lizard-like hips, and ornithischians having hips more like those of birds. The crocodiles and the pterosaurs rank equally with these two orders of dinosaurs. The common feature that saurischians and ornithischians share with each other (and with mammals) is that their legs were underneath their bodies, holding them upright and giving them more mobility than their sprawling reptilian cousins. Many dinosaurs, from both orders, could even stand and run on their hind legs.

Most – virtually all – paleontologists accept the term dinosaur, even though it has no place in the strict scientific classification. However, Robert Bakker and his colleague, Peter Galton, have gone a stage further. In the present classification system, the five classes are mammals, birds, amphibians, reptiles and fish. The two orders of dinosaur are divisions of the reptile class. The evidence that birds are descended from dinosaurs is, however, now very strong indeed, while the evidence that many dinosaurs were warm-blooded is, to say the least, persuasive. Dinosaurs, say Bakker and Galton, were more like birds than like any living reptile, so it is nonsense to classify them as reptiles. They propose revising the classification so that the five classes become mammals, dinosaurs, amphibians reptiles and fish, with the class Dinosauria subdivided into not only the Ornithischia and Saurischia, but also the Aves (birds – confusingly, modern birds are more like the 'lizard hipped' dinosaurs than the 'bird hipped' variety). The new classification hasn't caught on. We think this is a pity, not least because it highlights the fact that dinosaurs were much more like us, and other mammals, than like the reptiles we know today.

As Niles Eldredge, of the American Museum of Natural History, put it in his book *Life Pulse*, dinosaurs 'were the standard issue creatures of the day, and individual dinosaurs were as numerous as mammals are today' (p. 173). The 'terrible lizard' image of the dinosaurs conjures up pictures of creatures like *Tyrannosaurus rex*, and even when we remind ourselves that there were herbivorous dinosaurs as well (*Tyrannosaurus*, after all, had to eat something!) the first thing that springs to mind is an image of a kind of super-rhino, something like *Apatosaurus* (*Brontosaurus*), 25 metres long and with a body built like a tank. But there were also dinosaur equivalents of smaller mammals like wolves and goats. Chicken-sized dinosaurs must have eaten still smaller creatures (probably including our ancestors). Almost everywhere you look in the world today, if you see a mammal occupying a niche in the ecology and making a decent living out of it, you can be sure that there was a dinosaur equivalent filling much the same niche in the ecology a hundred million years ago. There is one obvious exception – ourselves and the other primates. How come, if dinosaurs were so successful, they never evolved intelligence?

The quick answer is that they had no need to – they got along very well without it, thank you, and the kind of environmental pressures that gave rise to human intelligence simply did not exist in the Cretaceous. More recent environmental conditions, as we shall explain later, put intelligence at a premium and hastened the emergence of our own species. Things were different in the Cretaceous; but is that answer really satisfactory? It is hard to believe that intelligence would not be an advantage for some species in any environmental setup, even though it might have emerged more slowly in more equable times. If so, it is even possible that intelligent dinosaurs might have appeared on Earth, sooner or later, had it not been for the catastrophe at the end of the Cretaceous that swept all large dinosaurs away, writing *finis* to the saga of Megadynasty III.

This 'might have been' has been developed by Dale Russell, of the National Museums of Canada, with the aid of a colleague, Ron Seguin. Their collaboration built from Russell's study, in the 1970s, of the fossil remains of a dinosaur specimen which had a relatively large brain, walked on two legs, and had four-fingered hands with opposable digits (the fact that our thumbs can 'oppose' each of the fingers on the same hand is what gives us the delicate grip needed for fine work, such as picking up grubs for food, chipping a flint to make an axe, threading a needle, or threading a nut on to a bolt). The ratio of brain to body weight of these creatures (with bodies somewhere between a turkey and an ostrich in size) placed them in the same range as large modern birds, or the less intelligent modern mammals. In 1977, astronomer Carl Sagan, in his entertaining and immensely popular book *The Dragons of Eden*, mentioned Russell's work and took things a stage further with the kind of speculative leap astronomers are famous for:

> If the dinosaurs had not all been mysteriously extinguished some sixty-five million years ago, would the *Saurornithoides* have continued to evolve into increasingly intelligent forms? Would they have learned to hunt large mammals collectively and thus perhaps have prevented the great proliferation of mammals that followed the end of the Mesozoic Age? If it had not been for the extinction of the dinosaurs, would the dominant life forms on Earth today be descendants of *Saurornithoides*, writing and reading books, speculating on what would have happened had the mammals prevailed? (p. 135)

Russell has described the reaction to this suggestion in his contribution to the book *Dinosaurs Past and Present* (edited by Sylvia Czerkas and Everett Olson). There was, he says with masterly understatement, 'a certain level of curiosity about what highly encephalized dinosaurs might have looked like' (p. 127). Russell and Seguin slaked that curiosity by building a model of the kind of creature that this dinosaur, which is also known as *Stenonychosaurus*, might have evolved into. They took its existing features, the large brain, upright posture and developing hand, and extrapolated their development forward into a mythical future in which the dinosaurs had not become extinct. The result, which they dubbed a dinosauroid, caused a sensation. Russell calculated that at the rate of evolutionary change going on in the late Cretaceous, a creature with a body weight the same as that of a modern human, and a brain to match, could have emerged within 25 million years (that is, 40 Myr before the present day), and the dinosauroid was built to match that forecast. The dinosauroid model looks more like a human being than a dinosaur, and Russell argues that this form 'may have a non-negligible probability of appearing as a consequence of natural selection within the biospheres of earthlike planets' (p. 130), because of the broad advantages conferred by, for example, the upright, bipedal posture (which frees the front limbs to develop hands capable of sensitive manipulations) and by the use of two eyes at the front of the head for stereoscopic (three-dimensional) vision to look for prey and to focus on whatever those hands might hold. 'The humanoid form may be a special (nonrandom) solution to the biophysical problems posed by intelligence' (p. 130).

Reaction to the idea has been mixed, as far as the experts are concerned, but some at least are favourable. Bakker, for example, says 'one could quibble about details, but Russell is probably correct in general. Moreover, those large-brained dinosaurs were certainly clever for their time, and probably hunted the rat-sized mammals of the period.' (*The Dinosaur Heresies*, p. 372). In 40 million years of further evolution, *after* they had achieved the equivalent of human intelligence, would the descendants of those dinosaurs have gone on to develop space travel and voyage to other planets, or would they have invented nuclear war and destroyed the Earth? Such speculations are science fiction (and, indeed, have been entertainingly developed by Harry Harrison in his *West of Eden* trilogy). Whether, like Bakker, you agree that such extrapolation makes sense, or whether, like one paleontologist we discussed this work with, you dismiss it as 'Dale Russell's fantasy', there is no doubt that it was a good thing for us that the day of the dinosaur ended when it did.

If there had been no great changes to the environment 65 million years ago, we would not be here now. Megadynasty II, dominated by proto-mammals and with more reptilian reptiles relegated to small-animal niches in the ecology, gave way to Megadynasty III, with the reptiles bursting out of their confinement and taking over, while mammals became scurrying, small creatures. Then, the roles were reversed once again in Megadynasty IV. If you feel bad about the way the dinosaurs treated our ancestors, you needn't; we take our revenge on the descendants of the dinosaurs every time we eat an egg for breakfast. When all the larger dinosaurs were swept from the stage (and by 'large' we mean everything from about the size of *Stenonychosaurus* upwards; if the intelligent dinosaur had been just a little bit smaller, the story might have turned out differently), mammals were able to diversify and compete for ecological space in the niches left vacant. Probably because of the abilities they had evolved, under the pressure of natural selection, in order to survive at all in a world dominated by dinosaurs, this time around they were able to beat any opposition roughly their own size out of sight, and take over the animal world, with many larger species evolving in the process. But what did kill off the larger animals at the end of the Cretaceous?

A unique catastrophe?

During the age of the dinosaurs, old continents broke apart and the fragments drifted around the globe, colliding with one another and re-arranging the geography until, by the late Cretaceous, less than 100 million years ago, the view of our planet from space would have been quite similar to the view seen by an astronaut today. The Atlantic Ocean was much narrower than it is now, and the Pacific was wider, with more freedom for warm water to circulate up into the North Polar seas. But it was recognizably 'our' planet.

The effects of all this on the forms of life that we find today were important. For example, 130 million years ago, although Gondwanaland was breaking apart there was still a land surface stretching from Africa and the Americas across Antarctica to Australia (and well north of the South Pole, which was covered by water at the time). Marsupial mammals (the ones with pouches) seem to have evolved in what is now Africa, and spread over this land bridge. In Africa itself, they were replaced by the modern mammals, the placentals; but by the time this happened the bridge to Antarctica-Australia had gone. The two southern continents remained a safe home for marsupials, with no competition from placentals until man arrived on the scene and brought his animals with him. Which is why kangaroos and the like are found in Australia today, although their cousins in Africa went extinct tens of millions of years ago.

What matters from our own point of view, though, is how the changing geography of the globe began to alter the environment in the second half of the Cretaceous. Studies of changes in the fossils of different species of sea-dwelling micro-organisms, the plankton, show the classic picture of a steady global cooling, with the extinction of many tropical species over an interval of several million years. Antarctica-Australia, breaking apart from Africa and the rest of fragmenting Gondwanaland further north, was drifting towards the South Pole once again, with all that that implied. Many species were in decline well before the termination of the Cretaceous – but many more disappeared very abruptly in a sudden extinction right at the end of the period.

It is the same picture on land. In several parts of the world, rocks from 65 million years ago show traces of a *sudden* change in plant life, a change which fits the idea of a rapid cooling of the globe, right at the end of the Cretaceous. But the fossils also show a more gradual change in land-based life for millions of years previously. Dinosaurs themselves dwindled over a span of at least ten million years, from 30 genera to 13 found in the fossil beds of Montana and southern Alberta. And the 'terminal event' wasn't all that terminal. Some researchers suggest that as many as nine species of dinosaur actually lived on into the next period of geological time, the Paleogene.[1]

---

[1] In the traditional geological timescale, the Cenozoic Era, which began 65 million years ago (and followed the Mesozoic Era), is divided into the Tertiary Period, from 65 Myr to 1.8 Myr, and the Quaternary, from 1.8 Myr to date. This is rather unbalanced, and some paleontologists now prefer to divide the Cenozoic into two more equal periods, the Paleogene, from 65 Myr to 24 Myr, and the Neogene, from 24 Myr to date. We go along with the modern timescale, but the terms 'Cretaceous-Tertiary', 'Cretaceous-

This decline may have been caused as much by a drying out of the continents as by the cooling that occurred. In the middle of the Cretaceous, although the land masses of the globe were getting closer to their present positions, the interior of modern North America and large parts of South America were inundated, and there was a huge shallow sea in the gap between North Africa and Eurasia, which has now dwindled to become the Mediterranean. All this water would have helped to give the land nearby an equable climate, like the climate of Britain today. But when the sea-level fell, as a result of tectonic activity, the shallow inland seas dried out and continental interiors, without the moderating influence of large bodies of water, became exposed to harsh winters and baking summers. This climate of extremes can have done no good to the vegetation or to the dinosaurs that fed on those plants. The picture that is painted, by paleontologists such as Steven Stanley, is of a world in decline, with both plants and animals, both in the sea and on land, suffering the consequences of a major (but slow) environmental re-arrangement, when something extra – meteor impact, outburst of volcanism, or both – struck at the already weakened populations. Eldredge, who has a knack for a snappy phrase, sums it up best: 'the role of an impact was to make a bad situation truly awful.' Without that last straw, perhaps the events of the late Cretaceous would have amounted to no more than a lesser extinction, with dinosaurs recovering afterwards, as they had four times before.

There is, indeed, evidence that an impact *did* occur at the end of the Cretaceous, and this may have been the crucial event that tilted the balance against the dinosaurs and in favour of the resurgent mammals. The extinctions at the end of the Cretaceous do not follow exactly the same pattern as the earlier extinctions we have discussed, and in particular there is some geological evidence that the world first warmed, then

Paleogene', and 'Mesozoic-Cenozoic' all refer to the same marker in the geological calendar, 65 Myr ago, when (most of) the dinosaurs died out. Since the first epoch of the Paleogene/Tertiary is called the Paleocene, in both classifications, the boundary can also be called the 'Cretaceous-Paleocene'.

cooled at the dawn of the Paleogene, while the sea-level dropped dramatically.

There are enough detailed 'explanations' of these events around to fill several books; we will pick just one, as an example as much of human ingenuity in thinking up disaster scenarios as of the susceptibility of Cretaceous creatures to climatic change. Michael Rampino and Tyler Volk, of New York University, linked several fashionable ideas together in 1988. They used evidence that 90 per cent of marine plankton was destroyed at the end of the Cretaceous. This is revealed by changes in the proportion of the isotope carbon-13 in carbonate rocks from that time. Levels of carbon-13 in those sediments did not return to normal for more than 300,000 years; the same sediments show a drastic reduction in the amount of calcium carbonate deposited, over a span of at least 350,000 years. As calcium carbonate is chiefly the remains of dead plankton, this confirms that little plankton was around at that time.

Whatever caused the extinction of plankton – and Rampino and Volk favour the impact of a meteorite – there should have been severe consequences for the climate. Supporters of the Gaia hypothesis – the idea that environmental conditions on Earth are kept more or less in balance by the action of living organisms – have recently become interested in the way plankton affect cloud cover. It sounds crazy – tiny organisms in the sea controlling *cloud cover*? – but it seems to make sense on closer inspection. Plankton produce large quantities of a substance known as dimethyl sulphide, or DMS. DMS gets into the air, where it reacts to produce the sulphur-bearing 'seeds' on which the water droplets that make up clouds can condense. Clouds, by and large, help to keep the Earth cool, by reflecting away incoming solar energy. Rampino and Volk calculate that removing 80 per cent of the plankton from the oceans would reduce cloud cover sufficiently to make the world warmer by 6°C, while a decline of plankton by 90 per cent would cause a warming of nearly 10°C. If that happened suddenly, as the result of a meteorite plunging into the sea, it would certainly disturb the balance of life on Earth!

It is an entertaining scenario, but not one we would want to push too strongly. (Less entertaining, but equally plausible, is the possibility that so much vegetation died and rotted as the inland seas dried out that the carbon dioxide concentration of the atmosphere rose and temporarily enhanced the greenhouse effect. The lack of carbonate sediments also tells us that carbon dioxide was not being taken out of the atmosphere; with no plankton around, the world warms even without the DMS effect.) Nobody knows exactly what happened. The fact that *something* unusual, and perhaps unique, did happen at the end of the Cretaceous is, however, borne out by another study published in 1988.

The question taken up by Thomas Crowley, of the Applied Research Corporation, in Texas, and Gerald North, of Texas A&M University, is whether climatic catastrophes in general can arise as a result of gradual changes, such as the drift of a continent over a pole, and whether the terminal Cretaceous event, in particular, fits that picture. They showed that you do not need an external cause – such as a meteorite impact – to produce abrupt environmental changes. There can be a discontinuous response, a sudden jump from one climatic state to another, as a result of slow variations in the background environment.

An example of this kind of change would be a steady increase, or decrease, in the carbon dioxide content of the atmosphere. The kind of sudden changes that can result are familiar from a branch of mathematics known as catastrophe theory. They happen if a system – in this case, the climate of the Earth – can exist in either of two (or more) stable states for the same external conditions. For example, with a particular amount of carbon dioxide in the atmosphere, and therefore a particular strength of the greenhouse effect, the Earth might be stable either without any ice caps or with a polar ice cap. Computer simulations show that this is indeed possible for some global geographies (perhaps including, interestingly, the present day geography of the globe) – with no ice cap, the climate is stable; but *if* an ice cap ever forms, it can maintain itself by reflecting away solar heat. In such a situation, the Earth might be ice-free, but with the potential for glaciation. If the carbon dioxide concentration then slowly declines, a point will be reached where the ice-free state is no longer possible. At that point, the system must flip into the stable state *with* an ice cap. *But,* and this is the nub of the matter, even if the carbon dioxide concentration now increases slowly once again to where it was before, the world stays glaciated, because there is no trigger to switch it back into the stable ice-free state.

When the two Texas researchers put some numbers into their computer simulations, they found that a change of this kind can occur for a temperature change equivalent to a variation of just 0.0002 per cent in the Sun's energy output. This is well within the range of variations that could be caused by changes in the carbon dioxide content of the atmosphere, or by changes in ocean currents caused by the changing geography of the globe. Two of the great extinctions of the past 600 million years, at the end of the Ordovician and in the late Devonian, fit this pattern extremely well, with a sudden onset of ice-age conditions following a long spell of ice-free climate; other extinctions we have mentioned fit the pattern reasonably closely. The extinction at the end of the Cretaceous, however, is quite different, because there is no evidence that the Earth flipped into a long-lasting glaciated state at that time, 65 Myr ago. The one big extinction where there is least evidence for this instability effect at work is the very extinction where there is reasonably strong evidence for an extraterrestrial impact. It really does look as if the terminal Cretaceous event was special – and we can put this in an intriguing context.

At the time the dinosaurs disappeared, the environment was in decline, and Antarctica was settling towards the pole. But the world had *not* yet entered an ice age. Suppose there had been no meteorite impact, or whatever, that made things awful instead of merely bad. Then, the dinosaurs might have recovered from the merely bad conditions. We know, from geological evidence, that a series of ice ages actually began about five million years ago, as the present geography of the globe became established. It would have happened anyway, and probably brought an end to the age of the dinosaurs (unless they had developed intelligence and a technological civilization) without the meteorite impact. It seems, on this evidence, that the Cretaceous actually ended 60 million years too soon. By rights, and from the evidence of previous extinctions, it should have taken that long for the climate to deteriorate to the point where massive extinctions occurred. The unique events of 65 Myr ago – which, tantalizingly, we may never be able to understand fully – brought a *premature* end to the age of the dinosaurs, and gave mammals an early start back up the road to prominence. By the time the ice arrived, 60 million years after the dinosaurs departed the scene, the mammals were ready for it. And that, literally, is where we came in.

3

The Return of the
Magnificent Mammals

By 65 million years ago, the main landmasses of present-day
North America, Eurasia and Africa were beginning to become
distinct continents, as the northern supercontinent known as
Laurasia began to break up. But the proto-Atlantic Ocean was
still a relatively narrow sea, closed at its northern end where
Greenland still snuggled between Europe and North America;
so animals could move reasonably freely across at least the
northern region of the supercontinent. In the south, the
equivalent supercontinent, Gondwanaland, still covered the
pole, with Antarctica more or less in its present position, but
with South America and Australia still attached to it. The
continuing breakup of Pangea, the old single landmass which
had formed 225 million years ago, and the re-arrangement of
the fragments, was to have a profound influence on the
changing climate of the globe over the next 65 million years,
and on the emergence of humankind. Sixty-five million years
sounds a short timespan, compared with some of the numbers
we have been bandying about so far. But to put it in some
sort of perspective, during the Cenozoic era half of all the sea-
floor of our planet has been recycled, crunched out of existence
underneath continents and born anew at spreading ocean
ridges. Since the seas cover two-thirds of our planet, this means
that one-third of the entire surface of the Earth has been
renewed since the death of the dinosaurs.

The seeds of our species, however, were already in existence
all that time ago, as the day of the dinosaur drew to a close.
We belong to the order of mammals known as primates.

Primates evolved through adaptation to a life in the trees; they include about 60 varieties (genera) of living animals (among them lemurs, monkeys, ourselves and other apes), and perhaps twice as many extinct varieties known only from their fossil remains (plus an unknown number of extinct varieties that have left no fossil remains for us to study). Life in the trees requires a different set of abilities to life on the ground, and over millions of years evolution has selected those advantageous characteristics in ourselves and our close relations. You need good physical agility and co-ordination in order to get about among the branches; good eyesight, in order to find food, look out for enemies and to see if the next branch you are going to grab on to is safe. Stereoscopic – three-dimensional – vision, so that you can judge distances and jump safely from branch to branch, requires that eyes should be at the front of your head with overlapping fields of view. The ability to hold on to branches with all four limbs (and preferably a tail as well) is essential, and at least a couple of those limbs have to end in hands that are capable of holding on to food, either to carry it to a place of safety or while it is being eaten. Drop a tasty morsel from a treetop, and you have lost your lunch for good. The variety of food available – some fruit, some insects, the occasional piece of meat – affected the evolution of primate teeth. While other varieties of mammal specialized in developing either sharp cutting teeth (for meat eaters) or big grinding teeth (for vegetarians), our omnivorous ancestors kept the full variety of teeth found in the ancestral mammal forms (incisors, canines, premolars and molars) in a fairly neat all-purpose package.

Finding all the variety of food, making use of the good eyesight and co-ordinating the agile limbs in running about in the trees all took a reasonably sophisticated nervous system, and so primates also evolved relatively large brains for their body size.

So we have an identikit picture of a primate – a mammal with a large brain, good stereoscopic vision (and good hearing), with good grasping hands and all-purpose teeth. Another characteristic feature, which probably evolved from the need to hold small babies safely in the treetops, is that female primates have a pair of milk glands on the chest. The whole package is, hardly surprisingly, recognizably human. The surprise is that creatures whose fossil remains show enough of these features for them to be classified as primates were already around 65 million years ago, in the region that is now Montana. (But then again, if ancestral primates were around at the end of the Cretaceous, it is no surprise that most of their descendants, after a further 65 million years of evolution, are so superbly adapted to life in the trees today; the interesting thing is the way some of those descendants – ourselves – have abandoned the archetypal primate lifestyle.)

In those days, the climate of Montana was very different from what it is today. To start with, North America was closer to the equator. In addition, as well as there being a gap between North and South America, there was an open seaway between Africa and Eurasia. So ocean water could circulate freely around the globe at low latitudes, while on the other side of the world from Laurasia there was a huge ocean with unrestricted access to the North Pole. All of this helped to keep the climate warm and equable. But as the fragments of Laurasia drifted further north, and as this and other factors helped to cool the climate, primates became restricted to the tropical zone – not so much because they couldn't stand the cold themselves (after all, they were furry and warm-blooded), but because they needed an all-year-round supply of fruit and insects to eat.

The megayears of boom

Although the oldest known primate fossil comes from North America, remains almost as old have been found in Africa and South America, and nobody can say exactly where or when our order began. But they must have been interesting times. Maybe, as we have seen, in the aftermath of a cosmic impact; and certainly at a time when the Earth's magnetic field (possibly as a result of that impact) went crazy. Between about 70 and 80 million years ago, there was just one reversal of the field; in the ten million years around the end of the Cretaceous there were at least 16 reversals. Nobody can be sure why this happened (though it seems likely that it was associated with the breakup of the supercontinents), or what effect it may have had on the climate of the Earth or on life; interestingly (and perhaps even alarmingly, if you take a very long-term view) the frequency of reversals has increased, erratically, over the ensuing 65 million years, with roughly 40 reversals occurring in the past ten million years. This increase in magnetic activity has accompanied a long, slow cooling of the globe – that may be a coincidence, but the cooling, at least, has played a major part in our story.

Mammals in general, not just primates, participated in the recovery of life from the catastrophes, whatever they were, that had brought an end to the reign of the dinosaurs. Not just the Cretaceous Period, but the Mesozoic Era, had ended; in the Paleogene Period (the first part of the Cenozoic Era) there were new opportunities for the survivors to multiply, evolve and adapt.

At first, just about all they did was multiply. Mammals spread out, and increased in numbers, but stayed fairly small and rat-like. But within a few million years, the first mammal boom was well underway. New species evolved to fill the niches left vacant by the demise of the dinosaurs, and in many cases this involved an increase in the size of the mammals, and the development of a bigger brain. At the same time, the supercontinents were breaking apart, so that some varieties evolved only in some parts of the world, and could not spread to other continents – the classic example is the evolution of marsupials, mammals that carry their young in pouches, across the southern supercontinent. Some of the early beneficiaries of the death of the dinosaurs were mammals that would look distinctily weird to modern eyes. Grazers, for example, that grew to look like sheep the size of rhinos – but not grazing on grass, which, although it emerged early in the Paleogene, did not spread to dominate large areas of the world until the end of that period, some 25 million years ago. Equally bizarre carnivores fed on these giant 'sheep', and mammals were again moving back into the seas from which their ancestors had come so long ago, producing several kinds of whale by the early Eocene, an epoch within the Paleogene that began about 58 million years ago. At around the same time, the continuing evolutionary activity on land saw the emergence of bats, true rodents and hoofed animals, including ancestral horses the size of modern dogs. By 50 million years ago, ancestral elephants the size of pigs were also on the scene.

From our point of view, though, the most important evolutionary development during the Eocene was the emergence, about 50 million years ago, of the first ancestral monkeys, a new variety of primate. Unfortunately, the fossil record of this event is sparse, and there is very little precise, direct information available about when and where the monkey line appeared. One of the most interesting features of this development, however, is that two kinds of monkey seem to have emerged separately, from the same kind of ancestral primate, in response to evolutionary pressures acting in the same way in diffferent parts of the world.

By this time, South America was isolated from the rest of the continents – except Antarctica-Australia, where there is no sign of monkeys. And yet, monkeys that look very similar to one another, and which occupy the same ecological niches in the forest, emerged both in South America and in Africa. The two groups – known today as 'New World' and 'Old World' monkeys – must have evolved independently from some earlier kind of primate, and yet their differences are quite superficial. The New World monkeys have developed a grasping tail, which they can use as a fifth hand, while the Old World monkeys can only use their tails as balancing poles; and there are differences in the nostrils of the two kinds of monkey. But those are the only two obvious ways to tell them apart. Their separate evolution shows that when the ancestral primate was set the evolutionary 'problem' of adapting to a particular environment, occupying an ecological niche in the trees of the tropical jungle and living off fruit and leaves, it came up with the same 'answer' twice. This is an example of what is known as parallel evolution. Within the 'gene pool' of primates – the DNA that we inherit from our ancestors – there is scope for a certain amount of variation and adaptation of the basic mammal form, and those changes that will occur by chance and be selected by evolution operate within those limits to tailor the outward physical form of a species to its niche. For example, natural selection might favour primates with either more or less hair; but a primate line cannot suddenly evolve feathers in place of hair.

The idea of parallel evolution, that species are tailored by natural selection to fit their ecological niches, is very much the sort of argument that leads Dale Russell to imagine that an

intelligent dinosauroid would look rather like a human being
– perhaps we should say, 'rather like a primate'. It also explains
why some species of small whale and dolphin, mammals that
returned to the sea relatively recently, resemble sharks, fish
whose ancestors never left the sea. In order to be an efficient
swimmer, you have to be a certain shape, whatever your
ancestors were. And if that still seems a little far-fetched to
you, we can digress briefly to look at an even more striking
example of parallel evolution at work, operating not just
within the confines of the primate gene pool, but in the gene
pool of the whole mammalian class.

Mammals that give birth to their young as, essentially, tiny
embryos, and keep them in a pouch until they are big enough
to emerge into the world at large, are called marsupials. Our
kind of mammal, that gives birth to fully formed young that
can, in many cases, run with the herd almost as soon as they
are born, are called placentals. (Some primates, and especially
humans, are a special case in which the young may still be
relatively helpless at birth and need more time to develop,
because of their large brains; we discuss this in *The One Per
Cent Advantage*.) Placentals are a more efficient form of
mammal, in terms of the evolutionary survival of the fittest.
We don't have to worry about why this is so, but it is a fact
that everywhere that placental mammals and marsupials have
come into direct competition with one another, the marsupial
form has died out. The evidence for this is particularly clear
from South America, where marsupial evolution continued
successfully until about three million years ago, when the land
connection to North America became established. As placental
species invaded from the north, marsupials were pushed back
and have been completely wiped out in the space of a couple
of million years.

Australia, though, remained cut off from the rest of the
world until very recent times, when people brought some
species of placental mammal to the island continent. And it is
full of examples of parallel evolution. The native Australian
marsupials include the equivalent of placental mice and rats,
animals called dasyures that look like cats, koalas that resemble
bears, and kangaroos that, although they look very different,
do the same 'job' in the ecology as deer and antelope. The
range of variation allowed by the mammalian gene pool seems

to have allowed both placental and marsupial mammals to respond to equivalent evolutionary pressures in the same way, in most cases. Only exceptions, like the kangaroo, have produced different physical forms to fit the same ecological niche. A dasyure looks like a cat for the same reason a dolphin looks like a shark – because it has to be that shape to make a living in the environment it occupies. Starting from the same kind of basic mammalian stock, and applying the same kind of evolutionary pressures, you generally get the same 'answers'.

But in spite of the fascination of delving into the story of the evolution of other lines, the only way to keep our present story manageable is to focus ever more closely on the line that leads to ourselves as we come closer to the present day. Among other things, that means ignoring what was going on in South America and Australia, and concentrating on the development of the primate order in Africa. For it was there that some monkeys became apes, and some apes became human beings. Old World monkeys were in place in the region of Africa that is now the Sahara Desert, but was then lush forest, between 50 and 40 million years ago. They lived in the northern part of what was then an isolated continent, with open sea between Africa and Eurasia. As both continents moved north, Africa was catching up with Eurasia, and eventually collided with it, welding the two continents together in a union that has persisted to the present day. But before that happened, the ape line had already evolved from monkey stock; and the whole mammal class had been through an upheaval of extinctions caused by a series of catastrophic events and a major change in the pattern of ocean currents and the weather of our planet.

Setback – and recovery

The crisis began about 40 million years ago, and spanned about eight million years, covering the later part of the Eocene and the early Oligocene, which began about 37 million years ago. A lot of evidence for changes around this time comes from studies of the fossil remains of creatures that lived (and died) on the sea-floor, such as molluscs. The extinctions that occurred mainly affected species and genera, not whole families and orders, but were still substantial. The most detailed information about the changes that occurred around this time comes from studies of microfossils, the remains of the tiny plankton that live in the oceans and whose chalky shells build up in the sediments on the sea-floor. They show that, apart from being less extreme, the changes in plankton around 40 Myr followed a very similar pattern to the extinctions at the end of the Cretaceous, with species that liked warmth disappearing from the scene. Just two million years later, a second pulse of extinctions swept through the surviving plankton species, and there is also geological evidence for a meteor or comet striking the Earth at about this time. The end of the Eocene Epoch may well have been brought about by a similar, though smaller, cosmic catastrophe to the disaster that struck the dinosaurs at the end of the Mesozoic Era. But this cannot be the whole story of the changes that took place in the early Oligocene, because there were still three more waves of extinction to come, culminating about 32 million years ago. By and large, species declined over a long period of time, with the recognized extinction 'events' merely being the culmination of a deterioration that was happening anyway. The whole pattern of changing life in the ocean, over the best part of ten million years, can best be explained by global cooling on a dramatic and sustained scale. In round terms, studies of changes in different kinds of marine organism, that lived at different depths in the sea, show that the average temperature of surface waters in the tropical Pacific Ocean fell from 23°C to 17°C, while the temperature of deep ocean water declined from 11°C to 5°C. And the effects of the global cooling show up in the traces left by life on land, as well.

Temperature changes on land are recorded by changes in fossil plant remains – seeds, spores, fruit and pollen, as well as leaves and larger pieces of plant. Before the changes that occurred at the end of the Eocene and in the early Oligocene, regions at all latitudes of the world, it seems, enjoyed the kind of climate we regard as tropical. But during this ten million years of cooling many tropical and subtropical species disappeared from higher latitudes. Forty million years ago, London was further south than it is now, about at the latitude of Madrid, or Washington DC, today. That helped to keep it warm, but still placed it some 40° north of the equator. The deposits known as London Clay, in southern England, contain a detailed record of the changes that occurred between about 40 and 30 million years ago, and show that although at the end of the Eocene the vegetation in that part of England resembled that of the Malaysian jungle today (found on the *equator*, at 0° latitude), by 30 Myr the pattern had changed to that of a temperate climate, still warmer than today, but with seasonal variations. Think of tropical jungle in Philadelphia today, and you have some idea of the size of the climatic shift that occurred at the end of the Eocene and into the Oligocene. Seasons, in fact, could be said to have been invented at about this time. For hundreds of millions of years previously, up to the end of the Eocene, there had been little difference in climate at different latitudes, and even at high latitudes there had been little variation in the weather pattern during the course of a year. But by 30 Myr, winters at high northern latitudes were distinctly colder than summers, with frosts, if not snow, becoming common. Even more dramatic changes were occurring, as we shall see, in Antarctica.

Life on land seems to have suffered two main extinction crises around this time, one at the end of the Eocene and one about 30 million years ago. Mammals were particularly affected by the first extinction, with many of the weird and wonderful varieties that had emerged in the post-dinosaur wave of mammalian evolution being wiped out, eventually to be replaced by newer and (to us) more familiar forms. (To put some of this in perspective, it helps to recall that the events we are now describing occurred rather more than 30 million years ago, about halfway between the present day and the death of the dinosaurs; the first wave of post-dinosaur mammals had a run on the evolutionary stage almost exactly as long as the run the second wave of mammals has now enjoyed.) Recognizable ancestors of giraffes, pigs, deer, cattle, camels and rhinos all made their debut in the Oligocene. Their emergence and evolution was influenced by the continuing changes in climate – and not just temperature. As the world had cooled, the sea-level had fallen, leaving continental interiors further from the sea and with a less plentiful supply of rain. With less rainfall, in many parts of the world thick forest gave way, at last, to open grassland. The world began to look like the modern world after about 30 Myr, and the animals in it, especially the mammals, began to look like modern animals.

As we have already mentioned, one of the modern lines that emerged from these upheavals was the ape line, descendants of the Old World monkeys that lived in northern Africa.

The monkey line itself continued to enjoy its old lifestyle, high in the trees, even though the size of the area covered by dense forests in northern Africa was shrinking. If the climate hadn't changed, and the forests had not shrunk and been replaced, in some regions, by more open woodland, there might never have been any ape-like variation on the monkey theme. After all, look at what happened to the New World monkeys in South America – nothing. There, because South America stayed as an isolated continent straddling the equator and drifted mainly westward and only a little north for tens of millions of years, lush jungle remained the order of the day, and the New World monkeys, superbly adapted to life in lush jungle, stayed as they were. Like the dog that failed to bark in the night, this is a persuasive piece of evidence, and lends weight to the view that it was the environmental changes in Africa that encouraged – or forced – some Old World monkeys to adopt a new kind of lifestyle, one which can be characterized, even for these earliest apes, as being built around a more omnivorous diet than that of fruit- and leaf-eating monkeys. Even in Africa, where the lush jungle remained, so did the monkeys; it is where the regular supply of tropical foodstuff began to disappear that some erstwhile monkeys, the evidence of fossil teeth shows, developed the ability to eat other foods.

There is other, circumstantial, evidence that the climate-related upheavals of the Oligocene were responsible for the emergence of the ape line. The fossil skull which has the distinction of being recognized as the earliest known remains of an ancestral ape comes from a region known as the Fayum Depression, in Egypt; in honour of this it is known as *Aegyptopithecus*. It was found in strata 28 million years old, dating from just after the upheaval, in the heyday of the second wave of mammals.

The 'first' member of the ape family (strictly speaking, still a pre-ape, not a genuine ape) was a cat-sized creature, a tree-climber with a supple back and long limbs, each ending in a grasping hand; it had a larger brain, compared with its body weight, than any other mammal known from that time. Of course, all this information was not gleaned from a single skull; other remains of *Aegyptopithecus* and its near relations have been found in slightly younger deposits, and by about 25 Myr there were several types of proto-ape around in northern Africa. Apes are distinguished from monkeys, in living species as well as in the fossil record, by several features. Apes tend to be larger than their monkey contemporaries, and although both climb in the trees monkeys run about on top of the branches while apes swing along beneath the branches (this shows up in differences in the structure of their skeletons, especially shoulders and hips, which are adapted to different forms of locomotion). Monkeys and apes have different teeth, reflecting their different diets; and apes have bigger brains and are more intelligent. There are other differences, but these will do to be going on with; they are certainly sufficient to pick out ape fossils from monkey remains, even in strata 25 million years old.

By now, we are talking about our very close relations indeed, members not just of the same order as ourselves (Primates), but of the same family (Hominidae, or hominoids). The hominoid family, in fact, contains only humans and other apes (the name *Hominid* refers only to ourselves and any ancestors that we do *not* share with other living apes); it took about 20 million years, after the emergence of monkeys, for the first apes to split off from the monkey line, and it wasn't until some 25 million years after the arrival of *Aegyptopithecus* on the scene that the line leading to *Homo sapiens* split from that of our sibling apes. This is another pointer to the importance of environmental, and especially climatic, changes in our evolution.

Apes appeared in Africa from the monkey stock at about 30 Myr because their environment changed; but then nothing much happened to the environment for more than 20 million years, so there was no pressure for any striking new development in the ape line. Steady evolution and adaptation to the new world that had emerged from the Oligocene upheavals was the order of the day, in our line as in others. The world had by now changed so much that geologists set the end of the Oligocene Epoch, and of the Paleogene Period, at 24 Myr, and from then on we are in the Neogene, the second period of the Cenozoic Era. The first part of the Neogene is called the Miocene Epoch, a relatively long subdivision of geological time which ended only five million years ago. The early Miocene, in particular, was the time when mammals came into their own. There were continuing geological changes, including the upheavals that created the Alps, and activity under the eastern part of Africa that was lifting a large area like a dome and would eventually crack it open to produce rift valleys littered with lakes and edged by active volcanoes. The steady drift of continents to different latitudes continued all the while. All this brought about a continuing shift to drier weather in many regions, and an expansion of grassland at the expense of forest; the new prairies were inhabited by a greater variety of mammals than has been seen on Earth either before or after the Miocene. Our class spread into every part of the globe, in great waves of migration, while our family diversified into several varieties of ape, some emerging from Africa to populate large areas of Eurasia as the two continents collided and were joined together. If any interval of geological time fits the description, this was when the world resembled the Garden of Eden. The new mammalian world, including the world of the apes, owed its existence to the final breakup of Gondwanaland, far away from Africa, and to the development of an ice cap over the South Pole as a result. Not just people, but all apes, are indeed children of the ice.

Winter in Eden

It was the cooling and drying of the globe in the Oligocene that created conditions that we regard as ideal, an Eden-like paradise on Earth. Such conditions seem so appealing to us because we have evolved and adapted to fit those conditions, just as the dinosaurs of old were evolved and adapted to fit a more 'tropical' planet. Had they been around in the Miocene, they would probably have hated it. But it was the invention of winter that made Earth an Eden for our family.

There is no mystery about either the timing or the cause of this change in climate. The changes in fossil remains of plankton in cores drilled from the ocean floor and brought to the surface for analysis show that the mass of cold, deep water that is a feature of the circulation of the oceans today only began to develop at the end of the Eocene, about 37 million years ago. The deep, cold layer developed because the Antarctic continent, over the South Pole, began to freeze about then. Very cold *surface* water at high southern latitudes would have been denser than the warmer water, and would have sunk down into the depths of the ocean before beginning its journey northward as a cold bottom current (just as hot air rises, so cold water sinks; and for the same reason – colder fluids are more dense than their warmer counterparts). The cold water sinking near the pole and moving to lower latitudes cannot stay deep forever. The pressure of more cold water piling in behind it eventually forces the current to well up in warmer parts of the world, bringing cold water to the surface and cooling even the tropics. Then, the cool surface water warms in the heat of the Sun as it begins its journey back towards the polar regions to complete the cycle. Such currents, orginating near both poles, are a feature of the ocean circulation today; but before the end of the Eocene, when the whole world was warm, they simply did not exist.

Independent evidence of the timing of the growth of glaciers in the Antarctic matches up with the timing inferred from plankton studies from the tropical Pacific sea-floor. There is some evidence that ice began to build up as early as 40 Myr, just when the series of Eocene–Oligocene upheavals began, and firm evidence that a full-scale ice sheet had developed in East Antarctica by the early Oligocene, at 35 Myr. The evidence comes from sediments of these ages that contain typical products of glacial activity – mixtures of clay, silt, sand and gravel – and which are dated by magnetic techniques. The outer edge of the ice sheet may have been as much as 140 kilometres beyond the present ice front, and the evidence from East Antarctica is mirrored by similar traces of glacial activity from the Ross Sea, on the western side of the continent. Whether or not cosmic impacts were involved as a 'last straw' effect, in some or all of the extinctions that occurred around this time, it is certain that Antarctic glaciation was the main cause of the change in climate and the long, slow decline of many species, including most of the first wave of post-dinosaur mammals. But why did Antarctica cool?

Before the end of the Eocene, Antarctica was still attached to both South America, on one side, and Australia, on the other. Warm ocean currents that flowed poleward from the tropics swept southward along the edges of both Australia and South America, cooled only a little as they moved past the edge of Antarctica itself, and then turned northward again to return to the tropics. But at the end of the Eocene Australia and Antarctica broke apart, with Australia beginning to shift northward, with its cargo of marsupials, to its present location (where it is not fixed, of course, but continues to drift northward). This allowed a new, cold current to develop, flowing through the widening strait between Antarctica and Australia. This cold current deflected the southward flow of warm water before it could reach Antarctica, building up a barrier between the southern continent and the warmth of the tropics. Now, the main current flowed southward down the eastern seaboard of South America, cooled at high latitudes, and travelled eastward almost around Antarctica, through the strait between Antarctica and Australia, before returning northward up the western side of South America. With this barrier current in place, even though South America was still attached to Antarctica, the land mass over the polar region began to cool, and ice began to build up, first over the land alone and then over the sea itself.

The growth of the glaciers may have been triggered simply by a slow cooling of Antarctica until some critical threshold was reached. Or, perhaps, one of those suspected early Oligocene impact events may have cooled the southern hemisphere enough for snow to begin to lie in a permanent layer over the continent. The cooling may have been hastened by minor shifts in the position of Antarctica, which placed the continent more centrally over the South Pole. Whatever the exact cause of the spread of the first snowfields, once snow did begin to lie over the land, a self-perpetuating southern ice age would have begun. The white, reflective layer of ice and snow bounces heat from the Sun back out into space, making the polar region much colder than it would be if there were no ice present, and encouraging the ice sheet to grow, and to chill the waters at the edge of the continent. Cold water could now sink into the depths to create the cold, deep layer of the ocean. This would have been a sudden change, whatever the exact trigger, and would have been disastrous for any inhabitants of Antarctica.

It is interesting to speculate on what kind of animal and

plant life might have lived there before the ice began to spread. After all, even without permanent ice cover the south polar region still experienced a long winter night, during which no plants could grow and there would be no food for animals. Perhaps there was highly seasonal vegetation, eaten by animals that migrated southward each spring and retreated towards Australia or South America, following the Sun northward, each autumn. But any evidence for their existence, and for a massive wave of extinctions in that part of the world when the ice arrived, is buried now beneath glaciers many kilometres thick. Some survivors may have emigrated to South America; on the Australian side of Antarctica, however, there was nowhere left to go, unless you were a strong swimmer.

In the middle of the Oligocene, around 33 million years ago at the time of the last great wave of Oligocene extinctions, geological activity deepened and widened the gap between Australia and Antarctica, making the cold current stronger and reinforcing the development of cold bottom water flowing north, ultimately to well up at lower latitudes. As well as evidence of the development of large ice sheets on land, the sea-bed cores from those times show that plankton adapted to cold conditions proliferated in the waters around Antarctica from then on. About 30 million years ago, just at the end of the period of Oligocene upheavals, the last connection between Antarctica and South America also broke. Antarctica itself was not immune to continental drift, but its main motion at that time (and since) was a slight rotation, an anticlockwise swing around the pole. At the same time, South America was (and is) moving westward. But the rotation of Antarctica was not fast enough to keep up with the drift of South America, and over millions of years the piece of land joining the two continents was stretched and bent, eventually breaking like a piece of stretched toffee. You can still see traces of the stretching and distortion of the rocks of the Earth's crust in any atlas which shows the region of the southern tip of the Andes and the horn of Antarctica; both westward-shifting pieces of continent have left trails of little islands behind them at the break, forming the Scotia Arc, but with the Antarctic horn lagging behind the tip of South America.

Once this final break with the rest of the world had occurred, Antarctica was surrounded by sea, and the current flowing eastward along its borders became a true circumpolar current, circling the entire globe. Looking down from above the South Pole, this is a great clockwise current. To the north, from this perspective the surface layer of the ocean circulation system is dominated by three great counter-clockwise currents, in the South Atlantic, the South Pacific and the Indian Oceans. The southern edges of these counter-clockwise currents blend in with the northern edge of the circumpolar current, like the teeth of three great counter-clockwise gear wheels meshing with the teeth of a clockwise rotating cog. Once the pattern became established, the whole circulation of the southern oceans acted to reinforce the strength of the circumpolar current and to strengthen the barrier, in the upper layers of the ocean, between the cold water around Antarctica and the rest of the world. Surface water could only get through to the edge of Antarctica in the form of eddies, the oceanic equivalent of low-pressure weather systems; and once it got there and cooled, it could only return to the tropics in the form of a deep, cold current.

The cooling of the south polar region had a direct influence on the climate of the globe, enhancing the difference between winter and summer and cooling the world generally as cold winds, as well as cold ocean currents, moved northward away from the pole. The root cause of this cooling was the fact that some solar heat that used to be absorbed by the Earth was now being reflected away by the ice sheets at the pole. There must also, though, have been an indirect, but perhaps even more important, contribution to the creation of winter in Eden.

The warmth of the world in the 20 million years or so following the recovery from the death of the dinosaurs really is astonishing, when compared with present day climate, or with the climate of the Miocene. Malaysian jungle in England, even allowing for England being a few hundred kilometres closer to the equator, is not something that you would expect to develop today even if the polar ice caps were removed. Nor, come to that, does it seem entirely plausible that a continent covering the South Pole, and subject to months of winter darkness, could remain entirely ice-free, whatever the ocean currents were doing. And yet, the geological evidence shows that it did, for 20 million years and more. Could some other effect have been warming the world in the first part of the

Paleogene? Almost certainly, yes. The obvious candidate is the carbon dioxide greenhouse effect, the process which traps, in the lower atmosphere, heat that would otherwise be radiated out into space by the warm surface of the Earth. When the atmosphere contains more carbon dioxide, then the world, other things being equal, is warmer. And, as it happens, the warming effect is stronger nearer the poles, where the input of heat from the Sun is weaker. The very richness of the vegetation in the early Paleogene hints that there may have been more carbon dioxide around then, since as well as sunlight plants need carbon dioxide for photosynthesis, and thrive when there is more of it available. The warmth of the world in those days makes it almost certain that there was a thicker blanket of carbon dioxide then. Since carbon dioxide is produced by volcanic activity there is no problem in explaining why there was more carbon dioxide in the air at a time when supercontinents were breaking apart, being torn at the seams along great rift valleys that were edged with belching volcanoes.

Today, although things are quieter on the geological front, natural volcanic sources still produce carbon dioxide (and so do human activities, as we discuss in chapter 8), but the amount of the gas in the atmosphere has stayed roughly constant for millions of years because natural processes take carbon dioxide out of the air and lay it down in sedimentary rocks, in the form of carbonate compounds. Those natural processes are driven by a kind of oceanic pump (with biology playing a part), in which carbon dioxide dissolves in cold water at high latitudes and is carried down into the oceans where plankton absorb it and use it to build their chalky, carbonate shells. When the plankton die, the shells fall to the sea-floor, and gradually build up layers of carbonate rock. Cold water is much more efficient at dissolving carbon dioxide than warm water, and this combined oceanic–biological pump is most effective at taking carbon dioxide out of the air and sequestering it in rock today at high latitudes, especially in the cold waters around Antarctica, which are rich in nutrients and where plankton thrive. But those cold waters were not there in the early Paleogene. Before the cold Antarctic waters developed, the carbon dioxide pump must have been less efficient; but when the flow of cold, deep water out of Antarctica became established, and the cold-loving plankton began to proliferate there, there must have been a sudden (by geological standards) draw-down of carbon dioxide out of the atmosphere, and a reduction of the strength of the greenhouse effect. As well as more solar heat being reflected away from the surface of the Earth, *less* heat was being trapped by the atmosphere on its way out into space. No wonder the world cooled in the Oligocene. The cooling was to continue, although much more slowly, right up to modern times. Although the mammals that proliferated in the Eden of the Miocene had no way of knowing it, it was to be downhill all the way, climatically, from then on.

The day of the ape

The mammal heyday of the Miocene was also the apes' heyday. *Aegyptopithecus*, the apes' precursor, emerged from the upheavals of the Oligocene almost 30 million years ago, but the fossil evidence reveals very little about what was happening to our close relations over the following ten million years. After about 25 Myr, however, there seems to have been an almost explosive radiation of ape varieties, and by now these were true apes, with all the important distinguishing characteristics that we have mentioned. The success of the apes over the next 20 million years or so coincided initially with a time when the world warmed slightly, compared with the Oligocene, but remained dry. The dry conditions, with a lower sea-level than before, were, of course, directly related to the establishment of a large ice cap over Antarctica. The size of the ice cap must have varied during the Miocene, but it seems that from the Oligocene to the present day there has always been some ice over the South Pole.   With the arrival of true apes on the evolutionary scene, this is probably a good place to stop and take stock of what evolution is all about. Many people, even today, have a vague idea of evolution as representing a climb up a long ladder, with ourselves at the top. The funny little, cat-sized *Aegyptopithecus*, and the apes of the Miocene, might be regarded, in that picture, as imperfect creatures struggling to achieve the perfection represented by humanity. Stated that baldly it sounds silly, and it is. Although the creatures whose fossil remains we study may have vanished from the evolutionary stage and become extinct millions of years ago, they were well fitted to the environment in which they lived at that time. Each creature in our own ancestral line was a success story in its own right, adapted to a certain lifestyle and occupying its own niche in the ecology. Indeed, there is no reason to single out the human line as special, except for our own chauvinistic interest in it – all the rest of the variety of life on Earth in the Miocene, or before, was an evolutionary success story in its day (just as, indeed, termites, budgerigars, salmonella bacteria and all the rest are equally as successful as ourselves today, by the only evolutionary criterion that matters, the fact that they are alive and able to reproduce). There is no way in which we can claim to be 'better' than *Aegyptopithecus*, or the Miocene apes – just different. They were well adapted to the world in which they lived, and we are well suited to the world in which we live. The reason why we are here now, and not them, is primarily because the world changed at the end of the Miocene, and created new evolutionary opportunities. The story of how and why that change happened will be told in the following chapters. But first we want to bring the story up to the end of the Miocene, five million years ago, and introduce the variety of apes that enjoyed the cool, dry conditions, with widespread open forest and extensive grasslands, of that epoch.

The closer we come in the evolutionary story to the emergence of our own species, *Homo sapiens*, the more the experts argue about the exact interpretation of each fossil and how it relates to ourselves. Fortunately, very often these are arguments only about details, and about who should have the honour and fame accorded to the discoverer of a 'missing link' or the 'oldest human ancestor'. The arguments don't obscure the underlying picture of human evolution, and we don't have to worry about the details of the debate here; but if you are interested in them we recommend Roger Lewin's entertaining book *Bones of Contention*. Out of all this debate, a relatively new understanding of the emergence of the human line has developed over the past ten years or so (a story detailed in *The Monkey Puzzle*, by John Gribbin and Jeremy Cherfas); from now on, we will be following this modern interpretation of our ancestry, and especially the summing-up in another book by Roger Lewin, *Human Evolution*. Some of the names and dates we mention may not quite fit with the story of human evolution you have read about in older books, or which you learned about in school, or even from Richard Leakey's popular TV series of a few years ago, *The Making of Mankind*. (Leakey himself has changed his views on the timing of key steps in the emergence of humankind since that series was made). But the overall picture we present here is an outline of the best and most complete understanding of the making of humankind that science can now provide.

The day of the ape began at the beginning of the Miocene, 24 million years ago. By 20 Myr, there were plenty of apes around in Africa, members of different species but grouped together by paleontologists under the overall name of dryopithecines – *pithecus* is the Greek for 'ape', and the prefix tells us that the creatures lived among the trees. The big radiation of the apes occurred a little later, however, when Africa nudged up against Eurasia and created a land bridge joining the two continents. Apes and relatives of modern elephants, among other species, spread out of Africa and into Eurasia; cats and horses, among others, moved the other way. There may have been changes in climate that favoured the apes' way of life around this time, or it simply may have been that they found Eurasia to their liking. Whatever the reasons, although monkeys also moved into Eurasia following the collision between the two continents about 18 million years ago, the apes diversified much more and spread into more ecological niches. In terms of species, around 15 million years ago apes outnumbered monkeys 20 to 1, judging from the fossil evidence, and there is neither any point nor any need to elaborate on all the places they went or all the varieties that developed. It is enough to say that apes were one of *the* success stories of the Miocene, and that the present handful of ape species on Earth, including ourselves, represents the pathetic rump of a once great family.

There are just three groups of apes from around this time that are of interest to paleo-anthropologists. One is known as *Gigantopithecus* (from the size of the fossil remains), and the other two as *Ramapithecus* and *Sivapithecus*, named after Hindu gods. Together they are sometimes known as 'ramamorphs'; they were sufficiently like the modern apes that *Ramapithecus*, in particular, was for a time thought to be our own ancestor, the first step along the line leading to human

beings from the basic ape stock. Remains of *Ramapithecus*
have been found in deposits as old as 14 million years and as
young as seven million years, so it was certainly a successful
variation on the ape theme (for comparison, *Homo sapiens*
proper has been around for less than 100,000 years, and the
uniquely *Homo* line, we now know, for about three million
years; in terms of longevity, as yet we are less than half as
successful as *Ramapithecus*). But the idea that Ramapithecus
was uniquely an ancestor of ours, and not of other modern
apes, has now been rejected. A combination of recent fossil
finds and new techniques for analysing the closeness of the
relationship between living species (including humans and other
apes) from studies of their DNA show that the split between
ourselves and the other African apes occurred even more
recently, less than five million years ago. *Ramapithecus* is now
thought to have been the ancestor of modern Asian apes, such
as the orang-utan. These are our evolutionary cousins, but we
are even more closely related to the African apes, the two
kinds of chimpanzee and the gorilla – indeed, by the usual
classifications, people *are* African apes, although we like to
think of ourselves as something special, in a category of our
own, the hominids. ('Hominid' is a term reserved for ourselves
and for any ancestors of ours that lived *after* the evolutionary
split with our nearest ape relations; 'hominoid' is a broader
category that includes other living apes and their immediate
ancestors).

Unfortunately, none of the many varieties of ape around in
the Miocene can be confidently identified as the ancestor of
the African apes. Although some members of the ramapithecine
line stayed in Africa while others migrated to Asia, through
the Miocene forests that stretched across the newly joined
northern landmass, the African branch of the family, according
to the conventional wisdom among paleo-anthropologists
today, seems to have died out, while some other, unknown
form of ape was flourishing – or, at least, *surviving* to leave
descendants, some of whom were our own ancestors. The
vagaries of the fossil record mean that we know of a variety
of creatures that were ancestral to both ourselves and the
ramapithecines around 20 Myr (the dryopithecenes), and we
have fairly good evidence about relations that may not have
been our direct ancestors but who lived from 14 Myr to

7 Myr (the ramapithecines); but on that standard picture none of the direct ancestors of the human line seem to have been preserved in fossil remains from about 18 Myr all the way down to 3.6 Myr. We have our own doubts about this standard interpretation, which we shall air in chapter 4; but the picture becomes much clearer after *Ramapithecus* has left the stage. The evidence from 3.6 Myr is for a distinctly hominid, not merely hominoid, ape, the earliest known direct ancestor of our own distinct line, separate even from that of the other African apes. All the signs are, though, that the split from the lines leading to the chimps and gorillas had only just occurred at that time, and that it had occurred because of another upheaval in the Earth's climate.

Downhill all the way

When Africa and Eurasia were welded together about 18 million years ago it marked the beginning of the end of the pause in the climatic deterioration, a pause that had made the first part of the Miocene marginally more comfortable for life on Earth than the Oligocene had been. Ocean currents flowing between the two land masses had helped to maintain equable conditions, but with this flow cut off, the climate in the heartland of Eurasia and in northern and eastern Africa became drier and more seasonal. This may have helped the early dispersal of the apes out of Africa, providing them with the kind of open wood (as opposed to tropical jungle) that their lifestyle was suited to; in the long term, however, as the trend continued and many regions became too dry for trees the changes would bring an end to many of the varieties of ape that flourished in the Miocene, and, indeed, to many other mammal species as well.

The pattern of life in the oceans changed significantly around 14 Myr. Although there had been ice at sea-level somewhere around the southern continent ever since 35 Myr (or even earlier), the amount of ice cover had varied; at 14 Myr, though, the Antarctic ice sheet expanded, and stronger deep, cold currents pushed their way northwards. It has remained fully glaciated ever since. With more water locked up in the great ice sheets, the world became drier still, and grasses came into their own in semi-arid regions of the globe. Around the same time, volcanic activity increased (perhaps because of collisions between pieces of the Earth's crust) and there is evidence of a moderately large cosmic impact in Europe. Many species of mammals, and even genera, disappeared at about this time, and most of the dryopithecine apes went extinct. But, as always at a time of evolutionary upheaval, some varieties survived and adapted. It may be no coincidence that the earliest known ramapithicenes, at 14 Myr, date from around this time.

There were few dramatic changes in climate over the next ten million years, and no major extinctions to rank with some of the catastrophes we have discussed, but a succession of relatively minor events mark the decline in climate. Mountain glaciers appeared in Alaska around nine million years ago, and left their traces in the form of scars in the rocks; at a little less than 7 Myr, glaciation spread to the mountains of South America; and by 6.5 Myr there was so much water locked up in Antarctic ice that the sea-level fell below the level of the neck of land joining Africa and Europe across the equivalent of the present-day Strait of Gibraltar. Over an interval of more than a million years, the entire Mediterranean Basin repeatedly dried out and refilled. The Mediterranean Sea today loses about 3,300 cubic kilometres of water to evaporation each year, and is maintained only by the inflow of water from the Atlantic; without that inflow, it would take just a thousand years to dry out, leaving a layer of salt tens of metres thick and, since the water evaporating there must fall as rain somewhere else, raising the average sea-level around the world by 12 metres. Cores drilled from the bed of the Mediterranean show several layers of salt produced in this way, evidence that the sea dried up several times. On each occasion, when the sea-level later rose sufficiently for water to break through again (presumably when the Antarctic ice retreated slightly), water would have thundered in at a rate of 40,000 cubic kilometres a year, 10,000 times faster than the present Niagara Falls, taking a hundred years to refill the basin. Geological activity, opening and closing the gap between Africa and Spain, may also have played a part in this cycle of Mediterranean droughts.

Whatever the exact cause of the desiccation of the Mediter-ranean, these changes must have had a profound effect on life in the region. When the sea dried up, there would have been little moisture available to produce rainfall over the land to the east of the Mediterranean basin, and this series of events may have been responsible for finally cutting the link between African and Asian apes, with expanses of desert lying between their two homelands (the link was also severed by the growth of great mountain ranges, including the Himalayas, as Africa continued to push northward and India also collided with Eurasia, beginning about five million years ago). The apes, and other species, of North Africa itself must also have been affected, with their woodland homes shrinking back into a heartland further to the south. It was just about at the time the Mediterranean sea settled into its present-day form, around 5.3 million years ago, that some ancestral form of ape that had lived through these convulsions, and whose own evolution had undoubtedly been affected by the accompanying climatic upheavals, gave rise to the three lines that would become ourselves, gorillas and chimpanzees. We can only guess at the exact nature of that ancestral ape, since no relevant fossils have ever been uncovered. But there is a wealth of evidence about how and where apes evolved into people over the next five million years, and about the climatic and other environmental changes that brought about this adaptation, driving our ancestors out of the wood and on to the plains. The previous chapter closed with the death of the dinosaurs, at the end of the Mesozoic Era and the Cretaceous Period; now, we have come to another logical place to break our story, not quite the death of all the apes, but certainly the end of the epoch of the apes, the Miocene. From now on, our tale is strictly that of the hominid line itself.

4

Out of the Wood

About five million years ago, the world once again changed sufficiently for geologists to set that date as the end of an epoch, the Miocene. The new epoch that began at that time is called the Pliocene; for us, this is the most special of all past geological epochs. During the Pliocene, the first true hominids appeared on the evolutionary stage; and by the end of that epoch our ancestors were already sufficiently human to go by the name of *Homo*. Yet this was a much shorter interval than the Miocene, lasting only up until about 1.8 Myr. (Because it is easier to find and interpret evidence from more recent subdivisions of geological time, there is a tendency for the size of each division recognized by the experts to be smaller the closer we come to the present; this does not reflect an increased pace of geological or evolutionary change, but simply that, just as when we view a broad landscape, we can see more detail close up.) On the old geological timescale, the Pliocene was also the last epoch of the Tertiary Period; in the new system of classification, it is simply the second of four epochs in the Neogene. But either way it is, in a sense, ours.

Our line emerged during, and because of, another shift in the climate. But this change was much more subtle and long term than some of the dramatic changes, accompanied by mass extinctions, that mark the boundaries of other intervals of geological time. Indeed, one of the curious distinguishing features of the Pliocene is that it was an epoch when a *deterioration* in climate brought about what seems at first sight to be a *proliferation* of mammal species. To understand this apparent paradox, we have to stand back a little and look at the broad pattern of geological changes going on over the past ten million years or so, and especially at the way the land masses were slowly drifting into their present-day positions.

Drifting into drought

Little was changing in the deep south of our planet around this time, except that Antarctica was becoming increasingly isolated as both Australia and South America moved away from it. This may explain why the circumpolar current intensified around 6 Myr, producing the waves of extreme cold that locked up more ice than today in the Antarctic, and caused the repeated desiccation of the Mediterranean Basin. At that time, the layer of ice over the southern continent was several hundred metres thicker than it is now, with sea-level some 50 metres lower than today and desert in Austria as a result. But while Antarctica's increasing isolation was locking it into a pattern of ice, wind and ocean currents that has persisted, with minor fluctuations, for many millions of years, the situation around the North Pole, where there had been open and relatively warm water since before the time of the dinosaurs, was changing.

As our attention focuses more finely on the evolution of the human line, we find that changes around the North Pole, not the South, come to dominate the story of the changing environment and its influence on our ancestors. Gradually, as continents moved northward into the Arctic zone, the climate in some regions changed. There is evidence of glaciation over the mountains of what is now Alaska as early as ten million years ago; this is an exception, linked with the growth of those mountains, and there is no sign of general northern glaciation until the end of the Pliocene itself. But it serves as a useful reminder both that conditions in the far north were getting colder, and that mountain building plays a significant part in altering the climatic patterns of the world.

Around the time that the Mediterranean Sea was drying up, the Arctic was enjoying a cool, temperate climate, with coniferous forests extending to the northern limits of the land. Those limits were actually further north than they are today, because the fall in sea-level that dried out the Mediterranean also left a broad expanse of continental shelf north of Alaska and Asia high and dry. By this time the continents were just about as far north as they are today, but this drying of the continental shelf pushed the boundary between land and sea several hundred kilometres northward of of its present position. There may well have been seasonal snows at these high latitudes, but there is no sign in the geological record of widespread permafrost at that time, nor for another couple of million years.

One factor that may have helped the north to remain largely ice-free for a little longer was an intensification of the Gulf Stream, a warm ocean current which flows northward up the eastern seaboard of North America, and carries heat to high latitudes. This is part of a circulation, or gyre, around the entire North Atlantic. The North Atlantic gyre itself may have intensified because of the changing geography of the globe, and especially as South America at last closed up on North America, with the gap between them being permanently bridged by about 3 Myr. Water that used to flow from the Atlantic to the Pacific between the two continents was increasingly diverted northward into the Gulf Stream as the gap slowly closed after about 5 Myr.

About the time that the series of Mediterranean desiccations ended (partly because the Antarctic ice retreated slightly, but probably also, since the Mediterranean has not dried out since, because of a geologically tiny widening of the gap between Spain and Africa), a new phase of mountain building was again reshaping the face of the planet. We have already mentioned that the collision between India and Asia began to build the Himalayas to their present magnificence about five million years ago; a little later the Andes Mountains of South America began to build upward from a relatively modest 2,000 metres height to their present 4,000 metres. As the Andes rose, they shielded the forests of the Amazon from rain-bearing winds (the prevaling westerlies), making the climate there drier. Similar changes occurred in the lee of the Himalayas, increasing the geographical differences in climate. Meanwhile, in the northern continents weather was becoming drier overall, but seasonal differences in climate were also increasing. The increasing strength of the pulse of northern seasons even extended its influence down into Africa, as the circulation of the atmosphere of the northern hemisphere began to shift rhythmically over the annual cycle.

Because there was a bigger variety of climates than there had been for tens of millions of years (at least), there was a greater variety of homes for life on the planet. When much of the land of the Earth was covered by what we think of as tropical jungle, then there was ample room for tropical species to live, but nowhere for any equivalent of modern temperate zone species to evolve. It was tropical forests or nothing. When the world became divided into tropical, temperate and other zones, that was bad news for the tropical species, who had their share of the real estate drastically reduced; but it meant that new species could evolve in different parts of the world as they moved out of the woods and adapted to fit the different conditions. So while the world became less of a tropical paradise for life, the *variety* of life on Earth actually increased. Modern dogs, for example, emerged about six million years ago, with bears, camels and pigs following in a spurt of mammalian adaptation and radiation over the next couple of million years. At exactly that time, as the jungle of Africa shrank, there was a three-way split in the line of the African apes. It happened in East Africa, where the local variation on the mountain-building theme was lifting a great slab of the Earth's crust and cracking it apart to create a great rift valley system. Instead of tropical jungle with a constant, all-year-round climate, the region became drier. The size of the rain forest was limited. While the amount of rain falling in any particular location depended on the new geography (whether or not the region was in the lee of a new mountain), overall the climate became slightly seasonal, as part of the pattern of global climatic changes. Islands of tropical jungle were now surrounded by grasslands and regions of more open woodland.

Tell-tale molecules

We know when the hominid line split from that leading to other African apes because molecular biologists can now measure the differences between the genetic material, the DNA, of humans and other apes (the technique is essentially the same as the 'genetic fingerprinting' that is now used to resolve disputes about paternity, and has been used to identify rapists and other criminals). This is part of the evidence which shows that *Ramapithecus* was not a hominid, but lived before the man-ape split. But some popularizations of the story of human evolution (and even some textbooks) fail to make the point that this does not necessarily mean that *Ramapithecus*, or at least one of the ramapithecines, could not have been an ancestor of *both* ourselves and the other African apes.

We described the biochemical techniques by which the genetic 'distances', as they are known, are measured in our book *The One Per Cent Advantage*. The essential point is that evolution proceeds because of the accumulation of changes in the DNA of species – changes in the genes themselves.[1] It happens that these changes occur at a more or less steady rate, at least in comparable molecules from closely related species. This is not something that you would necessarily expect to be true – people, for example, live longer than chimpanzees and have a greater gap between generations, so you might expect the molecular 'clock' to tick at different rates in the two species. But a battery of biochemical tests shows that this is not the case, and that the amount of change that accumulates in the DNA of human beings (their gene pool) over, say, a million years is roughly the same as the amount of change in

---

[1] We are, of course, aware that some people are still uncomfortable with the idea of evolution, especially when we start talking about specifically human evolution. The best brief response we can make to those who feel such discomfort is to paraphrase what Stephen Jay Gould, of Harvard University, said in an interview published in *Newsweek* on 29 March 1982. Evolution is a fact, like apples falling out of trees (the fact is attested to by, among other things, the wealth of fossil evidence alluded to briefly in this book). Darwin's theory of natural selection was put forward to account for the fact of evolution, just as Newton's theory of gravity was put forward to account for the fact that apples fall out of trees. Newton's theory of gravity has now been superseded by a better theory of gravity, the one developed by Einstein. But apples didn't stop falling out of trees when scientists began to debate whether Einstein's theory might be an improvement on Newton's. In the same way, some scientists now debate whether Darwin's theory of natural selection might be improved upon; but species don't stop evolving because of that debate, and the willingness of scientists to debate the mechanism of the process doesn't indicate that they doubt the fact of evolution.

the gene pool of chimpanzees over a million years.

These changes are all relative. They show, for example, that there is about a one per cent difference between the genetic material of human beings and either of the other two African apes, the chimp and the gorilla. The 'distance' between ourselves and the orang-utan is, in molecular terms, about twice as great, showing that the line leading to both ourselves and the African apes split from the line leading to the orang-utan (and the other Asian apes) roughly twice as long ago as the three-way split in the African ape line. If we can find just one accurate date from the fossil record, an accurate date for a split in the primate line, then all of the other dates in the sequence fall into place.

The date which is used to provide this benchmark is the date of the split between Old World monkeys and apes, the arrival of *Aegyptopithecus* on the scene just under 30 million years ago. The genetic distance between any of the living apes and Old World monkeys is about three times the distance between all the African apes and the orang-utan (perhaps a little more than three times this distance). So if the distance between apes and monkeys corresponds to about 29 million years of separate evolution, the difference between African apes and the orang-utan must correspond to about nine million years of evolution. By the same token, the difference between ourselves and the other two African apes corresponds to just half this, between four and five million years of independent evolution. The date for the human–ape split, inferred from the molecules in our blood, is smack in the middle of the time when the East African forests were fragmented and in retreat, with the region drying to provide new habitats in the form of open woodland and grassy savannah. We can date the emergence of the hominid line to within about a million years, even though we have no fossil remains of our ancestors from exactly that time.

The big split between Asian apes and African apes occurred between eight and nine million years ago, as the Miocene climate deteriorated and the forest linking the two groups disappeared. *Ramapithecus*, of course, was still around in both parts of the world at that time, and had been since at least 14 Myr. So there is no problem in accepting the fossil evidence that *Ramapithecus* was the ancestor of Asian apes such as the orang-utan. But did the African branch of the *Ramapithecus* family really die out? The molecules tell us that we share a common ancestor with Asian apes from about 10 Myr. The ancestor of the Asian apes that was around at 10 Myr was *Ramapithecus* (or, at least, a ramapithecene). So it seems entirely likely that our own ancestor from 10 Myr was also *Ramapithecus* – indeed, it is difficult to see any other interpretation that matches both the fossil and the molecular evidence.

Ramapithecus disappears from the African scene at around 7 Myr, not that long before the date of the human–ape split. As the molecular technique has been refined in recent years, so the dates of this particular three-way split have been adjusted. Some researchers still argue that there was an almost simultaneous branching of some ancestral (ramapithecine?) line into lines leading to ourselves, chimps and gorillas. But other tests, using proteins from the tissue of living individuals, as well as their DNA, suggest that the gorilla line split off first, at around 8 Myr, and that the split between us and the chimps occurred a little later, at 5 Myr. The fit between the disappearance of *Ramapithecus* and the emergence of the gorilla line seems almost too good to be true, but is nonetheless impressive. Just maybe, it means that we really do have a more or less complete fossil record of our own ancestry all the way from the dryopithecines at 20 Myr up to the final split with the chimps at 5 Myr. We don't have fossils from between 4 Myr and 5 Myr to confirm this interpretation of our ancestry. But the timing given by the molecules exactly matches the timing of upheavals caused by the changing climate. And we know *where* the hominid line began, because there are plenty of relevant fossils from the region of the East African rift just a little later, between 3 Myr and 4 Myr. They show that the region had suddenly (by geological standards) filled with several varieties of 'ape-men' (in fact, one of the key discoveries is of the remains of an 'ape-*woman*'), our own ancestors and their very close relations. This radiation of the ape line must have been a response to the changing environmental conditions. But before we look at how those changing conditions drove our ancestors out of the wood, we ought to take stock of the almost bewildering variety of hominoid species that shared this corner of Africa at that time.

The entry of the hominids

The confusion is not helped by the way in which paleo-anthropologists keep arguing about the names that should be attached to different fossils, classifying and re-classifying species not quite at whim but in accordance with a set of rules sufficiently esoteric to leave most lay-people floundering. We shall try to stick to one set of names, without going into too much detail about the historical reasons why they were chosen. If you find different names attached to the same species in other books, don't worry too much about it. We will also pick out, from several different ideas about just how these different species were related, the view that, in our opinion, provides the simplest explanation for the emergence both of the hominid line (leading to ourselves) and of the chimp and gorilla lines.

The earliest hominid that is given the genus name *Homo* was around in East Africa by 2.5 Myr. Dubbed *Homo habilis*, this was an ape that walked upright (standing about 1.2 metres tall), had a fairly slight build and a large head with a brain averaging 675 cubic centimetres in size, just half that of a modern *Homo sapiens*. By 1.5 Myr, this had developed into *Homo erectus*. Taller (1.6 metres) and with a larger brain (925 cu. cm.), this was the species that spread the *Homo* line out of Africa and into Asia. Both species were tool users. By 500,000 years ago, *Homo erectus* had evolved into *Homo sapiens*, the modern human form that spread around the world. But the story of *Homo* is for the rest of this book.

Homo habilis shared the region of the rift valley with two very close relations, members of a genus called *Australopithecus*. *Australopithecus africanus* was the first on the scene, and fossils of this species have been found in strata 3.5 million years old. The youngest known fossils of *A. africanus* are dated at 1 Myr. They, too, were upright walkers with a slender build, about the same size as *Homo habilis*, but with a smaller brain, only 440 cubic centimetres in volume (not much different from the average for modern gorillas, about 500 cu. cm.). There is some evidence that *A. africanus* were tool users, but if so the tools were unsophisticated compared even with the stone tools used by *Homo habilis*. The other species of *Australopithecus* contemporary with *Homo habilis* was bigger and more heavily built, and is known as *A. robustus*. They were around between 2 Myr and 1 Myr, but no younger fossil remains have been found. Some members of *A. robustus* stood 1.6 metres tall, and their average brain size was a little bigger than that of the average modern gorilla, about 520 cubic centimetres (the biggest gorilla brains, however, check in at about 700 cu. cm.). But there is no evidence that they used tools.

Both the *Homo* and *Australopithecus* lines had emerged by 3 Myr, clearly descended from a recent common ancestor, but equally clearly two separate branches of the evolutionary tree. Where did all these creatures come from? And how were they related? The debate on those issues raged for decades among the experts – and, indeed, it still continues. But the answers may have been found in Ethiopia in the second half of the 1970s. There, Donald Johanson and colleagues discovered, over a lengthy period of fossil hunting, the most complete skeleton of any human ancestor more than 35,000 years old. Informally known as 'Lucy' (after the Beatles song *Lucy in the Sky with Diamonds*), the skeleton is 40 per cent complete, the remains of a female ape-person from about 3.3 Myr. She belongs to a species that was given the formal name *Australopithecus afarensis* in 1978, after much heart searching by the discoverers, who would dearly have liked to place her in the genus *Homo*. It remains a moot point whether *A. afarensis* or *H. afarensis* is the better name, but the simplest interpretation of the available evidence is that the species Lucy belonged to was ancestral to both *Homo* and *Australopithecus*. She walked, the structure of her skeleton shows, if not completely upright then certainly better than a chimpanzee walks today, and she stood just over one metre tall (other members of what may be the same species from the same site were as much as 1.7 metres tall, suggesting to some researchers that males towered over females), but she had a small brain – the best instant image of Lucy is of a proto-human body with an ape's head on top of it. Walking was, it seems, quite literally the first step on the road to being human; the big brain that we are so proud of came later, perhaps because of the opportunities provided by upright walking to free the hands for complex tasks (such as tool making) that needed a good brain.

Astonishingly, at about the same time that Johanson's team

were uncovering the remains of Lucy in Ethiopia, a thousand miles away in East Africa Mary Leakey discovered the actual fossil footprints made by a similar creature walking upright over a layer of volcanic ash that had formed about 3.7 million years ago. They were preserved by a remarkable series of coincidences. First, a volcanic eruption spread a layer of ash rich in carbonatite, a kind of natural concrete that sets solid if it is first wetted and then dried. Then, a shower of rain dampened the ash, and while it was still wet what Roger Lewin calls 'a veritable menagerie' of creatures hurried over it (perhaps fleeing from the eruption). Hares, baboons, antelopes, two types of giraffe and a kind of elephant were among at least twenty different species that left their marks in the 'concrete' before it set – along with two hominids joining in the exodus. Then, the hardening layer of ash was covered by more ash and by windblown dust and soil, remaining covered up until weathering exposed it to view in 1976. The hominid footprints that were revealed must have been left by very close relatives, anthropologically speaking, of Lucy. They were made by a large hominid and a small one walking side by side, and in the light of Johanson's discoveries it is tempting to guess that they were a male and a female of the same species, *Australopithecus afarensis*. But this is only a guess.

Indeed, there is still a great deal of guesswork and argument about the significance of all these finds. We don't want to go into all the details – Roger Lewin has already done that, in *Bones of Contention*. What we are interested in now is that both the fossil remains of Lucy herself and the presence of these fossilized footprints show that our ancestors set out on the path to becoming human by learning (or being forced) to walk upright. At the same time that some of the descendents of *A. afarensis* were improving their walking skills and developing bigger brains, two other descendents, *A. robustus* and *A. africanus*, seem to have died out. At least, that is the conventional wisdom. But there is at least a possibility, which we discussed in *The One Per Cent Advantage*, that these two australopithecine lines actually survived and evolved to become modern gorillas and chimpanzees. In order to make the pieces of the puzzle fit together in this way, you would either have to adjust the molecular timescale a little (which is possible, but not easy), or you have to accept that the split between our line and the two australopithecine lines contemporary with *Homo habilis* occurred rather before Lucy's day, so that she is really a member of *Homo afarensis*. The second possibility seems quite likely, in view of the molecular evidence that the human–ape split occurred at around 5 Myr; but the puzzle then is why there are no fossils of *A. robustus* and *A. africanus* from around Lucy's time.

In any case, at present we are stuck with the official name *Australopithecus afarensis*, and if that is what the experts have decided it seems logical to place the split (with some slight misgivings, and acknowledgement that other interpretations are possible) after Lucy. Fortunately, this is very much a side issue from the story we have to tell here. Whatever happened to the australopithecines, and whatever formal name you give Lucy, we can now see, from the evidence of climatic upheaval in East Africa around 4 Myr, just why our ancestors gave up the life of tree-dwelling primates and tried their luck out on the plains. Putting it at its simplest, it wasn't so much that Lucy and her like left the forests, but that the forests left them.

The bipedal brachiator

The East African Rift Valley System actually runs all the way from southern Turkey to the mouth of the Zambezi river, through Israel, the Red Sea and the lakes of East Africa itself. In places, the valleys associated with the system are 80 kilometres wide and 300 metres deep; and it is laced with active volcanoes. The system is the growing product of the same kind of plate tectonic activity that smashes continents together to throw up great mountain ranges – or, rather, the *opposite* kind of activity. Along the jagged line of the Great Rift, the Earth's crust is being torn apart by sideways forces associated with long, slow turnover of fluid material in the hot depths below. These are the same kind of forces that tore apart Laurasia and Gondwanaland, creating the present continents and setting in motion the present phase of continental drift. In a hundred million years from now, there may be a great ocean separating the bulk of Africa from the horn of Ethiopia and Arabia, newly formed sea-bed whose growth matches the destruction of old sea-bed at other sites around the world, especially along the western edge of the Pacific. But for the present, and in the immediate geological past which is of special interest to the story of human origins, the most important feature of the African part of the Rift Valley system is that it provides an enormous variety of habitats. There are dramatic changes over a short geographical range, providing an environmental patchwork, because of changes in altitude and in rainfall and water drainage patterns over short distances. Instead of a uniform spread of tropical jungle, patches of dense forest are interspersed with more open woodlands and grassy savannahs.

How does a tree-dwelling primate adapt when the forests in which it lives begin to shrink? There are two obvious solutions. Either you retreat into the heart of the forest, and carry on your business of finding food to eat and a safe place to sleep as before, or you step out into the new surroundings and try to make a living in a new way that suits the changing world. Without the individuals concerned making any consicous choice along these lines, this is the way that evolutionary pressures work to select new varieties from a common ancestral stock at times of environmental change.

There is no need, we are sure, to labour the point – you see what we are driving at. When the forests shrank, some apes became more 'ape-like', sticking with the trees and, if anything, becoming more efficient at finding resources there in the face of increasing competition for dwindling resources. Their descendants are the gorillas. Other apes, originally members of the same species, scrambled a living in the more open woodlands nearby, still among trees (although not thick forest), but forced to find food on the ground as well. As evolution fitted them better for this lifestyle, they became chimps. And a third branch of the family, perhaps descended from the individuals who were *least* adept at the old lifestyle and were pushed out on to the plains by competition from their cousins, had to find a completely new way to live, or die. They developed upright walking, were forced to eat almost anything that came to hand, and learned the value of sharing their food amongst a family or larger group. Eventually, they developed large brains, and became human.

All this must have been a gradual process. Stating it so baldly makes it sound like an overnight transformation – with one bound, the primitive ape leaped out of the forest, stood upright and became human. In fact, the adaptation is gradual – unnoticeable from one generation to the next, but building up over hundreds of thousands of generations, and millions of years of time. The apes that 'stayed apes' need not actually have retreated into the shrinking jungle – they were probably the ones that happened to live in the bits of jungle that were still there after the environment changed (and remember, this time the climate changed *slowly*). The apes that 'became human' did not physically move out of the jungle, but over a long period of time the climate in the valleys where particular groups of apes lived dried out and the trees slowly disappeared. In each generation, individuals that learned to cope with the changing conditions a little better than their contemporaries would be the ones that found most food and had the best chance of rearing offspring. If upright walking, for example, made it easier to find food and carry it back to the family, then natural selection would favour upright walkers, and the characteristic bipedalism of the human ape would evolve.

One interesting piece of corroborative evidence, that it was the changing climate that made humans out of apes, comes from the monkey line, from which we split almost 30 million years ago. Since the heyday of the apes in the first half of the Miocene, monkeys have been far more successful than we apes, in terms of the number of species around on Earth, and the handful of ape species today is greatly outnumbered by more varieties of monkey than you can shake the proverbial stick at. But monkeys, too, are primarily tree dwellers, and when the forests declined at the end of the Miocene, in some regions monkeys also had to adapt or die. At just about the same time that the hominid, chimp and gorilla lines were getting started, between 4 Myr and 5 Myr, the modern baboon line split from an ancestral monkey stock. Baboons are monkeys that have adapted to a life on the open plains, and use trees only for refuge. Humans and chimps represent the apes' 'answer' to the problem of shrinking Pliocene forests; baboons represent the monkeys' 'answer' to the same problem. But baboons, unlike people (and unlike Lucy) cannot walk upright. It may be that the world today is dominated by an ape-descended species, rather than monkey descendants, for one main reason – the fact that the lifestyle of a tree-dwelling ape gives it a body structure that, coincidentally, contains many of the features appropriate for standing, and walking, upright.

The point is that whereas monkeys are relatively small, light creatures that run along the tops of branches, and leap from tree to tree, apes are relatively large, heavy creatures, that swing hand over hand *under* the branches, and also swing, rather than jump, from one branch to the next. This means of locomotion is called brachiation. Of course, monkeys *can* hang from a branch by their hands (although they never move along the branch while dangling in this way); and an ape *can* scramble on top of a branch, if it finds one sturdy enough. But the habitual lifestyles of the two primates are different, and the structure of their bodies reflects evolutionary adaptation to these different means of locomotion. It only takes a moment's thought to appreciate that brachiation and, literally, hanging around in trees, favours the evolution of an upright body structure. Hanging from your own two hands, or standing on your own two feet, the basic position of your body is the same. Our brachiating ancestry is clear from many anatomical features of human beings, features which we do *not* share with monkeys. For example, you can bend your wrist in a right angle in the direction of your little finger – an obviously useful degree of flexibility when swinging through the trees. And you have (potentially) strong biceps, that, if you bother to keep in training, can lift you up on to a bar fixed overhead. Human shoulder joints allow far more freedom of movement than their monkey counterparts – and so on, and so on. Try kneeling on all fours, and you will find that the only view you get, unless you force your head back painfully, is of the ground; standing upright, your head is ideally placed for looking around – but the position of the head on top of the spinal column is also just right to give a good field of vision to an ape hanging by its arms from a branch. So – we are descended from brachiator stock, and the anatomical adaptations required by brachiation and evolved over millions of years in the Miocene already suited the ape body, in many ways, to the task of standing upright. Lucy was such a good walker that her ancestors (possibly ramapithecines, or ramapithecine stock) must themselves have already begun to move out of the woods and on to the plains. We have seen why they, and their descendants, *had* to make a go of a new lifestyle in a changing world. But *how* did their rapidly developing ability to walk upright make them successful in that new environment, a couple of million years *before* they evolved into big-brained *Homo habilis*?

An upright stance offers many advantages out on the plains. For a start, it gives you the best possible view of your surroundings, both to find food and to get advance warning of predators coming your way. Secondly, once bipedal loco-motion has evolved, it is a more efficient means of getting around on the ground than the scrambling gait of the chimpanzee, and uses less energy. But most important of all, many paleo-anthropologists agree, it frees the hands to carry things. The 'things' might be weapons, even if these are only stones that are thrown to bring down a food animal or to scare off attackers; but perhaps the best explanation of the success of the upright lifestyle is that it enabled our ancestors to carry a variety of different kinds of food, gathered here and there, back to the family group to share. There is archeological evidence from sites in East Africa two million years old that by then our ancestors were spending a lot of time at certain locations. They left behind them discarded stone tools and bones from many different kinds of animals – animals which certainly didn't just wander into the camp and drop dead, but whose bones, still covered in meat, were carried there by people. Those lumps of meat, however, may have been a minor part of the group's diet. Unfortunately, any seeds and food plants that were brought into the camp for consumption have left no fossil remains; but there are other ways to find out what this kind of lifestyle involves.

Tribes that lived in much the same way, hunting for some of their food and gathering plants to share as well, at a settled site, survived in some parts of the world until well into the twentieth century, and their lifestyle has been studied by anthropologists for clues as to how our ancestors lived. There is a typical division of labour between the sexes in such hunter–gatherer societies, with males sent out to hunt while females look after the children and gather plants to eat. Lest we be accused of rampant sexism in pointing out this basic fact of human life, we should also emphasize that the males are not necessarily very good providers – the group usually depends on the women and the food plants they gather for survival, with the occasional contribution of meat from the men a welcome bonus. Only slightly facetiously, some observers quip that the main reason for the men being sent out hunting is to keep them out of the way while the women get on with the real work. But this tongue-in-cheek comment conceals the important truth that by making different individual efforts to find different kinds of food the group as a whole (and the individuals who are part of the group) has more chance of survival, because each individual is not dependent on a single source of food that might, for whatever reason, be unavailable one particular day or during one season. As for the hunting itself, this certainly began merely as scavenging, picking up on the leftovers from the kills made by the really efficient hunters, such as the big cats.

Early humans may not have been *very* good at anything, except walking upright; but they managed, with the aid of their upright stance, to make a reasonable job of doing each of a lot of different things. They became unspecialists. But whatever the exact sources of all the different foodstuffs needed to make the unspecialist, food-sharing lifestyle work, the key requirement is the ability to carry things back to camp to share. You need hands to carry things, and that only leaves you with two limbs free for walking.

Before even becoming intelligent, the human line became a bipedal brachiator. The change to bipedalism happened in response to changing climate and environmental conditions in the Rift Valley system of East Africa; but for several million years bipedalism gave the erstwhile brachiators a successful lifstyle *without* the need for intelligence. What was it that forced the bipedal brachiators to become intelligent, after about 2 Myr? Almost certainly, another turn of the climatic screw − or rather, several turns. By 3 Myr, the ice had begun to spread in the north. At first, the onset of the northern ice age had little impact in East Africa. But its influence began to be felt more strongly, and in an unusual way, just at the time that *Homo habilis* was emerging. Around the end of the Pliocene and the beginning of the Pleistocene, 1.8 million years ago (at the beginning of the Quaternary Period on the old timescale), there was a dramatic decrease in the rainfall of the region, linked with the spread of ice at high latitudes. This heralded the onset of a series of ice age rhythms that brought unique environmental pressures to bear on the bipedal brachiators. The children of the ice were about to appear on the African scene.

5

A Man – and a Woman – for All Seasons

If it had not been for climate-related environmental changes, we would still be Miocene apes living in the trees. The first phase of cooling in the northern hemisphere and drying in Africa was sufficient to push our ancestors out of the woods and make them upright walkers. But the series of climatic changes that put a premium on intelligence, and set us on the road to being human, were much more subtle and complicated than a mere cooling of the globe. They turned an ape (albeit an upright ape) into *Homo sapiens* in less than three million years – a breathtakingly fast spurt of evolutionary change. This happened in response to a climatic situation that is extremely rare, and may even be unique, in the long history of our planet. But it was only in the past couple of hundred years that the intelligent ape realized that the climate of the Earth had recently been through a series of convulsions, now known as an ice epoch; and it was only in the present century that we first appreciated that this ice epoch began a couple of million years ago.

The idea that great glaciers had once covered large parts of Europe that are now ice-free occurred to several people in the late nineteenth century. Before that time, observers of the natural world had already noticed that so-called erratic boulders are sometimes found in places where they don't belong, far from any rock formations that they match, and that the landscape of parts of Europe is dotted with jumbled heaps of rocks and sediment. To most seventeenth-century geologists, however, it was 'obvious' that this was the work of the biblical flood, washing all before it. So it is ironic that in 1787 one of the first people to make the case that great sheets of ice, not a flood of water, were responsible was a Swiss clergyman, Bernhard Kuhn. Other scientists came up with similar ideas independently, and these included the Scot, James Hutton, who visited the Jura mountains of France and Switzerland in the 1790s; he was impressed by the scars caused by glacial activity that he saw in the rocks there. Hutton's espousal of the idea of an ice age also contains a minor irony. It was Hutton, after all, who first promoted the idea that the surface of the Earth had been shaped not by biblical catastrophes, such as the flood, but by the same processes that we can observe at work today, operating slowly over long periods of geological time.

This idea, the principle of uniformitarianism, implied a much greater span of Earth history than the timescale inferred from a literal interpretation of the Bible, and stirred controversy in the late eighteenth and early nineteenth centuries. Today, a modified form of uniformitarianism, and a long history of the Earth, are cornerstones of geology; and yet, as we have seen, the Earth does suffer catastrophes, as well, on the appropriate timescales. And one of those catastrophes is the ice epoch whose importance Hutton was one of the first to appreciate. Of course, there is no real conflict with his ideas of uniformitarianism, since the key phrase is 'on the appropriate timescale'. On a long enough timescale, catastrophe is 'normal'; in terms of the long history of the Earth, an ice epoch is one of the natural processes of change that shape the planet, like the action of volcanic eruptions (also pretty catastrophic, if they happen alongside you), or erosion by running water and tides. But neither Kuhn nor Hutton, nor anyone else of their generation, made much effort to persuade the scientific world of the time that there really had been an ice age. It was only in 1837 that Louis Agassiz, the 30-year-old president of the Swiss Society of Natural Sciences, took up the case and promoted it with such vigour, in the face of almost equally vigorous opposition from biblical catastrophists, that by the middle of the 1860s the ice age theory had become widely accepted.

Evidence of ice

The evidence that persuaded Agassiz that ice had scoured the European landscape was all about him in his native Switzerland. But his eyes were opened to the meaning of the marks of glaciers on the mountains by the work of Johann von Charpentier, a pioneering glaciologist who had been born in Freiberg (now part of East Germany) in 1786. Von Charpentier moved to Switzerland, later adopting the French version of his name, Jean de Charpentier (and later still, in 1855, he died there). He worked as a mining engineer, becoming director of salt mines in the canton of Vaud. He was intrigued by glaciers and impressed by their power. Working sometimes with other amateur geologists (including a civil engineer, Ignatz Venetz-Sitten, who introduced him to the puzzle), von (or de) Charpentier made a special study of the locations of large boulders which seem to be made of rock from the Swiss Alps, but are found today far away down the Rhône valley. By 1834, he had reached the conclusion, like others before him, that these huge, 'immovable' boulders could only have got there by being carried in the grip of great glaciers that had, long ago, slid down from the mountains during an ice age. He presented his evidence that year to a meeting of the Society of Natural Sciences, but seems to have persuaded nobody, including Agassiz.

Indeed, when young Agassiz heard of de Charpentier's work, he not only didn't believe a word of it, but set out to prove that the whole idea was nonsense. He was well placed to do so, since in 1832 he had been appointed Professor of Natural History at the University of Neuchâtel, and he was becoming known as an expert on fossil fishes. As a native of Switzerland, he was sure from every-day experience that glaciers could not move far enough, or fast enough, to transport great boulders down into the Rhône valley. As a good scientist, he set out to prove his case. To this end, he established an observing station in a hut on the Aar glacier, and carefully measured the movement of the glacier (and others) by driving stakes into the ice and measuring their movement. Confounded by the discovery that the ice moved much faster than he had thought, and persuaded that it could also carry large boulders along with it, Agassiz was converted from sceptic to believer and, like many converts, he became an enthusiastic evangelist for his new beliefs.

He started, in 1837, by dragging his reluctant fellow members of the Society of Natural Sciences out of the lecture room and into the mountains to see the evidence for themselves. They were not immediately convinced, and some even preferred to argue that marks in the rocks might have been made by the wheels of passing carriages, not by the grinding of boulders carried by glaciers. But Agassiz was not to be dissuaded. He went out with Venetz and de Charpentier to look at the evidence further afield, but soon raced ahead of them in his enthusiasm, propounding a wide-ranging theory of a world covered by ice, which he published in 1840. De Charpentier himself, unable to ride the whirlwind that he had helped to generate (and more than a little miffed by the way Agassiz had run off with the ball), only published his own version in 1841. But even if he had beaten Agassiz into print, there is no doubt which version of the story would have made more impact. When Agassiz wrote about ice ages, nobody else could rival his use of dramatic imagery, which gives even the tabloid journalists of today a run for their money:

> The development of these huge ice sheets must have led to the destruction of all organic life at the Earth's surface. The ground of Europe, previously covered with tropical vegetation and inhabited by herds of giant elephants, enormous hippopotami, and gigantic carnivora became suddenly buried under a vast expanse of ice covering plains, lakes, seas and plateaus alike. The silence of death followed . . . springs dried up, streams ceased to flow, and sunrays rising over that frozen shore . . . were met only by the whistling of northern winds and the rumbling of the crevasses as they opened across the surface of that huge ocean of ice. (cited by Imbrie & Imbrie in *Ice Ages*)

They don't, alas, write scientific papers like that any more (indeed, few scientists did in the 1840s). Although Agassiz did get just a little carried away, and (as we shall see) life did not completely disappear from the face of the Earth (or even Europe) during the ice ages, it was that knack for imagery and publicity that helped Agassiz to convince his colleagues that the evidence for ice ages had to be taken seriously. But he would have had no case to make, of course, if painstaking pioneers like de Charpentier had not tracked down and studied the huge erratic boulders. And even then, it took the best part of 30 years, and a lot more evidence, to persuade the doubters.

The evidence came in from around the world. In 1852, the awesome extent of the Greenland ice cap was mapped for the first time; later in the nineteenth century the size of the Antarctic ice sheets became known. And meanwhile more traces of the activity of long-gone glaciers were found not just in Europe but in North America. We know now that a ridge of glacial debris, 50 metres high in some places and marking the southern limit of the latest advance of the ice, runs all the way from Long Island in the east to Washington State in the west. In 1846, Agassiz himself visited the United States to study such remains of glacial activity; he stayed on as Professor of Zoology at Harvard University, married Elizabeth Cabot Carey in 1850, and remained a pillar of American science until his death in 1873 at the age of 66.

Ice over the Earth

In the second half of the nineteenth century, and into the twentieth century, the full extent of the great ice sheets of long ago gradually became clear. Over a period of several million years, huge areas of land around the north polar region of the globe have been scoured by ice sheets. But there was never a single, continuous sheet of ice uniformly distributed around the pole. The Arctic Ocean was covered by a skin of ice, just as it is today, and the southern limit of this ice reached much further into the Atlantic than at present, so that both Greenland and Iceland were set in a frozen sea surrounding them on all sides and stretching away to the south. Both these islands, indeed, were completely covered by their own glaciers – more than completely covered, in a sense, because as the sea-level fell (because water was locked up as ice) there was more dry land around the islands, and at the edge of continents, on which the ice sheets could rest.

The glaciers of the Alps, which left the traces that led the pioneers to realize there had been an ice age, were, ironically, relatively small beer by ice age standards, isolated (but large) mountain glaciers lying well to the south of the Eurasian part of the northern ice cap. This region of glaciation, known as the Scandinavian ice sheet, covered about 6.6 million square kilometres over present day Europe, from Britain in the west across the Baltic to modern Russia. It also pushed northward over the Arctic sea-bed to link up with glaciers in Spitzbergen, adding another half million square kilometres to its area, and linked with Siberian glaciers to the East. But in the farthest eastern regions of what is now the Soviet Union, there was no ice cap, because the world was too dry and no moisture-laden winds could penetrate there to dump their burden of snow.

The dry region continued across a land bridge between Asia and North America, where the Bering Strait had dried out as the sea-level fell. Most of Alaska was free from ice. But the greatest of all the ice age glaciations (the Laurentide ice sheet) covered all of Canada and a large part of North America. The southern limit of the ice ran roughly from the site of New York City to the Rocky Mountains in Montana, and it covered an area of more than 13 million square kilometres, a bigger area, on its own, than the Antarctic ice cap today (although not as thick as the present Antarctic ice). The Rockies themselves poked up through the ice, but another glacier system ran between them and the Pacific – 2.3 million square kilometres of ice in a ribbon from Alaska to Washington, Idaho and Montana. The southern edge of ice ran roughly through modern Cincinnati, Ohio; through St Louis, Missouri; past Kansas City, Missouri; and across St Pierre, South Dakota. On the other side of the world, ice covered the locations of Dublin, London, Amsterdam, Berlin, Warsaw, Kiev, Moscow and Leningrad.

Ice cover also grew in the southern hemisphere, although less extensively. Antarctica itself had, as we have seen, long since been in the grip of ice, and could hardly become more glaciated. But mountain glaciers expanded considerably in both South America and in New Zealand (especially the south island) at various times during the past few million years.

Many smaller glaciers gripped regions such as Tasmania and Japan, and spread over the mountains of China, as well as the mountainous regions of Europe and the Rockies south of the Laurentide ice sheet.

In North America and Eurasia south of the ice, the climate was both cold and dry. But, like the evidence of increased glaciation in the southern hemisphere since the end of the Pliocene, this is of only peripheral interest to our story. The key factor is that when the northern ice advanced, the weather also became dry (and a little cooler) in East Africa. There, climatic changes associated with the growth of great ice sheets to the north had a direct effect on our ancestors, the bipedal brachiators. In order to relate events in East Africa to climatic changes further north, it is crucial to have a timescale of the ice epoch. Not only to relate the beginning of the ice epoch to the changes further south that helped to drive our ancestors out of the woods, but also because the ice did not just arrive, one day two or three million years ago, and sit there quietly until about 10,000 years ago. Instead, it advanced and retreated in rhythmic waves of glaciation, producing a long, slow pulse of climatic change that put intelligence at a premium and made us human.

Ice age rhythms

The Pliocene ended, and the Pleistocene Epoch began, when ice first spread to cover a large part of the northern hemisphere. Nobody can set a precise date to that event, but we can say why it happened. It happened because the jostling of the northern continents in their drift around the globe and to higher latitudes finally sealed off enough of the flow of warm water into the Arctic Ocean for the skin of that ocean to freeze. Once it froze, it reflected away incoming solar heat in summer, and caused a severe chill to spread across the land nearby.

Although there are traces of Alaskan glaciation even from Miocene times, there was no significant advance of the ice in the north until the late Pliocene, a little over three million years ago. But then there are signs of glacial activity in Iceland, and other evidence of a buildup of ice. By 3 Myr, the Arctic region may have been nearly as cold as it is today, and although the snow and ice had still to spread further afield, a pronounced cooling and drying began in equatorial regions about this time.

Ice first appeared on the continent of Europe about 2.5 million years ago, about the same time that local glaciers formed on the mountains of California. There is no direct evidence available of the onset of glaciation in Greenland – or rather, if there is any evidence it is all buried under the ice cap today. But it seems likely that the glaciers began to grow there about the same time that they began to grow in nearby Iceland. Over all this period – indeed from 5 Myr to 2 Myr – the Antarctic ice cap was bigger than it is today, and sea ice, especially the Ross Ice Shelf, extended further out from the continent. But temperatures in Europe were still a little higher than those of today, and because the mountains were not so high as they are now rainfall penetrated more effectively into the heart of the continent than it does today, encouraging the spread of forests. Some time between 3 Myr and 2 Myr, however, the fall in sea-level shows that the amount of water locked up as ice in the Greenland and Antarctic ice caps combined was more than the amount of ice in the polar regions today. At present, the area covered by ice is about 15 million square kilometres. At the height of Pleistocene glaciation, the area covered was 45 million square kilometres, and the volume of ice reached 56 million cubic kilometres. Some people set their definition of the date of the *start* of the present ice epoch as when ice cover first exceeded that of the present day. Geologists, however, prefer to mark the beginning of the Pleistocene (which for most practical purposes is synonymous with the ice epoch) from a convenient reversal of the Earth's magnetic field that occurred 1.8 million years ago, and left its mark in rocks around the globe.

By a happy coincidence, this is almost exactly at the time of the earliest known fossil remains of *Homo erectus*, the first member of the *Homo* line to move out of Africa. In terms of the evolution of our own line, the arrival of *erectus* on the scene would in itself make a good excuse to date the start of the Pleistocene as just under two million years ago. Distinctly more human than its predecessor, *Homo habilis*, a typical early member of *erectus* had a brain with a volume between 800 and 900 cubic centimetres, and later specimens have cranial capacities as great as 1100 cubic centimetres, getting close to the present day human average of 1360 cubic centimetres. *Erectus* had more modern teeth, and a less prominent jaw than *habilis*, and 'below the neck', says Roger Lewin, '*Homo erectus* was essentially human, except in the substantial robusticity of the limbs and muscle attachment points and in having a slightly shorter stature.' (*Human Evolution*, p. 53). It was a fully erect (hence the name), upright biped that spread throughout Africa, Asia and Europe.

The *Homo* line emerged during the early phases of northern hemisphere cooling, before the ice had really taken a grip on Europe and North America. But the glaciers began to spread at mid-latitudes by about 2 Myr, just before the somewhat arbitrary date of the beginning of the Pleistocene. *Homo habilis*, the ancestor of *erectus* and the descendant of Lucy, was on the scene then, and had, in a sense, been created by the changing climate which had brought the spread of conditions unsuited to woodland apes. But just as the early phase of cooling and drying of climate was only a transition from an ice-free northern hemisphere into a state of full glaciation, so *Homo habilis* was only a transitional species from the australopithecenes (including Lucy) to *Homo*. It takes time for natural selection to produce an evolutionary response to a change in the environment, and hardly surprisingly the changes in the *Homo* line lag a little behind the major changes in climate – but only a little.

Remains of *habilis* are found from about 2 Myr to 1.6 Myr. The line changed so quickly, producing *erectus* from the *habilis* stock, because the climate continued to change, and because after about 1.8 Myr it was changing in a different way. For at least three million years, there had been a slow decline of climate in the northern hemisphere, a slide into an ice epoch that made its influence felt further south as a progressive drying of East Africa. But about the time that *Homo habilis* made a brief appearance on the evolutionary stage, the first wave of full-blown northern glaciation had given way to a new, rhythmic pulsebeat of climate in which the glaciers advanced and retreated many times. During the Pleistocene, the northern ice repeatedly expanded to the point where roughly 30 per cent of the entire land surface of the Earth (including Antarctica) was covered by a blanket of ice, and just as many times the northern ice retreated into its Arctic fastness, where it is today. This regular rhythm has only been fully understood since the middle of the 1970s, partly because, for more than a hundred years after Agassiz finally persuaded his colleagues that there had been 'an ice age', nobody had fully appreciated just how many separate 'ice ages' there have been during the ice epoch of the past 1.8 million years.

At first, it was difficult enough to persuade the scientific community that there had been one ice age. Then, as geologists began to examine the heaps of rock and other traces of glaciation in Europe and America, they realized that the ice had advanced not once but several times. By the early twentieth century, it was generally agreed that there had been four major ice ages over the past half million years or so, each lasting for, perhaps, a few thousand years, and with the ice ages separated by much longer intervals of warmth. Since the most recent ice age ended around 10,000 years ago, this was a fairly comforting picture. But the development of better techniques for dating geological remains and new techniques for determining the temperature of the Earth in years long gone by eventually overturned this cosy picture. It now seems that another ice age may, by geological standards, be imminent.

One of the key developments that led to this realization is a technique known as the 'isotope thermometer'. It depends on the fact that atoms of common elements in the environment, such as oxygen and hydrogen (which together make up molecules of water) come in different varieties, known as isotopes. Take oxygen as an example. Most of the oxygen in the air that we breathe and the waters that cover the world is in the form of atoms of oxygen-16, where the number indicates their weight. A small, but significant, minority are in a form known as oxygen-18, chemically identical, but two units heavier (one unit, on this scale, is the weight of an atom of hydrogen, the lightest element). A molecule of water that contains an atom of oxygen-18, instead of oxygen-16, is correspondingly heavier and will find it harder to evaporate out of the ocean than its lighter counterpart, but will more easily condense in rain or snow. At the same time, tiny creatures that live in the sea (planktonic foraminifera) use oxygen from their surroundings, among other things, to build the chalky calcium carbonate of their skeletons. Because the temperature of the water in which they live affects their metabolisms, the proportion of oxygen-18 that these creatures absorb depends on the temperature of the water. When the creatures die, their calcium carbonate skeletons sink to the bottom of the sea, building up layers of chalk. By drilling long cores from the sea-bed and extracting samples of different ages (which means from different layers) for analysis, geologists can use the varying amount of oxygen-18 in the sediments as an isotope thermometer that reveals how the temperature of the upper layers of the ocean, in which the animals that made those skeletons lived, has varied.

All this, of course, is very far from easy. Even extracting long cores of chalky sediment from the sea-bed requires sophisticated drilling technology, and analysing the cores by measuring isotope ratios is a painstaking business – not to mention the care needed in dating the cores, with the aid of their fossil magnetism and other geological markers. Although the idea was first proposed in 1947, by Harold Urey of the University of Chicago, it wasn't until the mid-1970s, three decades later, that a reasonably accurate chronology of recent ice ages was established (the full story up to that point is told by John Imbrie and Katherine Palmer Imbrie, in their book *Ice Ages*). Since then, the technique has been developed further, confirming and extending the picture that emerged in the 1970s. The technique will always be a little imprecise, both in terms of the exact temperatures and the exact dates it yields; but it can certainly tell the difference between an ice age and the warmth of the world today. Instead of four ice ages separated by much longer intervals of such warmth, we now know that there were certainly six ice ages in the past few hundred thousand years, and well over a dozen full ice ages during the past two million years. Not only were there more ice ages than used to be thought, each one lasted longer. Each full ice age, with ice and snow covering 30 per cent of the land surface of the globe, lasts for about 100,000 years (this is a rough figure; some ice ages are 'only' 70,000 or 80,000 years long); the intervals of warmth between ice ages, like the conditions we live in today, are called interglacials, and last for only about 10,000 years (this figure is equally rough; some interglacials may last as long as 15,000 years). We live in an interglacial that began about 15,000 years ago and in which the ice had fully retreated from mid-latitudes by 10,000 years ago. This is the basis for gloomy forecasts that the 'next ice age' is due; the occurrence of so much climatic variation over a period of two million years or so is why the whole long interval of cold is best referred to as an ice epoch, although the glaciers have advanced and retreated many times within that interval.

The idea that there had been 'an ice age' only became widely accepted in the 1860s, and the idea that there had been so many ice ages only became accepted in the 1970s, more than a century later. But it didn't take anywhere near as long to explain the new discoveries – indeed, in a sense it took no time at all. The discovery of the rhythmic pulsebeat of climate over the past million years or more needed no new theory to explain it in the 1970s, because a detailed explanation of why climate should vary with a rhythm 100,000 years long, with short interglacials dividing much longer ice ages, already existed, and could be traced back in its first detailed form to the work of a Scottish thinker who published his first paper on the subject in 1864, just as the ice age theory itself became respectable. His name was James Croll. His work on ice ages, and that of a later pioneer, Milutin Milankovitch (who developed the idea even further, and lent it his name) was ignored as long as 'everybody knew' that there had only been four ice ages in the past half million years, and that ice ages were much shorter than the intervals of warmth that separated them. When what everybody knew was overturned by the isotope thermometer in the 1970s, the theory of Croll and Milankovitch was ready and waiting to come in out of the cold.

The theory that came in from the cold

Like Agassiz, Croll followed in the footsteps of earlier pioneers. The idea that changes in the Earth's orbit as it moves around the Sun might influence our climate can be traced back to Johannes Kepler, a seventeenth-century astronomer (see Appendix). But it was Croll, in the 1860s and later, who first fully developed a version of the astronomical theory of ice ages, and Milankovitch, in the first half of the twentieth century, who refined and completed that theory by including all the relevant astronomical influences. Neither of them had an easy time, although for different reasons. But although neither lived to see it, in the end their efforts were vindicated by the isotope thermometer.

James Croll was born in 1821, and spent the early part of his life in a little Scottish village. His family worked a small piece of land, but this was not enough to support them. Croll's father worked chiefly as a stonemason, travelling to where there was work, so that young James saw little of him. At the age of 13, James had to leave school and work on the farm; his formal education ceased at that point. But he read widely, and encouraged by his mother he studied books on philosophy and science. In his book *Climate and Time*,[3] published in 1875, Croll later recalled that although self-taught, he reckoned that by the age of 16 he had a 'pretty tolerable' knowledge of the basics of 'pneumatics, hydrostatics, light, heat, electricity and magnetism'. But the farm could not support him, and now he had to find a career. Hoping that the work might appeal to someone who enjoyed studying theoretical mechanics, he became a millwright. It was a mistake, for, as he said, 'the strong natural tendency of my mind towards abstract thinking somehow unsuited me for the practical details of daily work.'

That comment sums up Croll's life. At the age of 21 he returned to the family home, gave up the trade of millwright, and concentrated on studying algebra. To eke out a living while he did so, he became a carpenter, and found, for once, that the work suited him – only to be forced out of it by the lingering effects of an elbow injury he had suffered as a boy, and which was aggravated by the work. Later, he would recall that the injury was what set him on the road to scientific achievement, and that had it not been for the stiff arm 'I should in all likelihood have remained a working joiner'. Instead, he now tried a succession of occupations that were less demanding on his elbow, and which also gave him more time to read and think. He worked in a tea shop, eventually opening one of his own, and found time off from his reading to marry, as well. When the business failed, at least partly

[3] Other quotes from Croll are from the same source.

because of his obsession with the wrong kind of books, he tried running a hotel. It is an indication of his lack of business acumen that he chose one in a Scottish town which already had 16 inns serving a community of 3,500 people, and, an abstainer himself, refused to serve whisky to his customers.

By 1853, Croll was an insurance salesman, a job he loathed. But four years later that too came to an end, when the Crolls were forced to move to Glasgow so that James's wife, who was ill, could be looked after by her sisters. A period of obviously blissful unemployment followed, during which Croll completed a book, *The Philosophy of Theism*, and actually managed to find a publisher for it, in London. Incredibly, the book was a modest academic success, and Croll made a small profit from it. Then, in 1859, he found his true niche in the world.

Croll became a janitor at the Andersonian College and Museum in Glasgow. 'I have never,' he said, 'been in a place so congenial to me.' The pay was poor, and the work menial. But the job gave Croll two things he prized above all else – time to think, and access to a first rate scientific library. He began to publish scientific papers, at first on electricity and other problems in physics. But by the middle of the 1860s, as geologists became convinced that there had indeed been an ice age, there was a great debate about what might have *caused* the Earth to cool. Croll became interested, and read up on the astronomical theories, ideas based on changes in the Earth's orbit. He improved on those calculations, and published his first ice age paper in the *Philosophical Magazine* in 1864, at the age of 43. The paper attracted attention, and Croll was urged to take his work further. He did so to such good effect that by 1867 he was offered (and accepted) a post with the Geological Survey of Scotland, and in 1876 he was elected a Fellow of the Royal Society.

The work which enabled a museum janitor to rise to the very top of the scientific tree developed the idea that as the Earth moves around the Sun there are long, slow changes in its orientation, which alter the amount of heat arriving at different latitudes in different seasons. We see such effects every year. The Earth is tilted in space, lying over at an angle of about 23.5° to the perpendicular to a line joining the centre of the Earth to the Sun (this angle itself varies, one of the components of the astronomical model of ice ages). When one hemisphere is tilted towards the Sun, it is summer; but at the same time the opposite hemisphere must be tilted away from the Sun, and there it is winter. The difference between summer and winter is very much like the difference between an interglacial and an ice age; could orbital effects account for that change, as well?

Croll calculated how the amount of heat arriving in summer and winter has varied over thousands of years, as the Earth wobbles, like a spinning top, in its orbit around the Sun. He found a regular pattern of changing seasonal temperatures, and he inferred that ice ages would develop in the northern hemisphere when the effects conspired to produce cold northern winters. In fact, this inference is wrong. Cold northern winters do not trigger the spread of ice. Paradoxical though it may seem, the improved timescale of ice ages provided by the isotope thermometer, and modern calculations using high speed computers, show that cool *summers* are more important for the spread of ice. The logic of this is quite straightforward.

With the present geography of the globe, there is *always* snow in the northern hemisphere in winter, but it melts in summer today. If summers were a little cooler, however, some of the snow on the ground might last the whole year round, building up, year by year, into great ice sheets. The more the snow and ice spread, the cooler the world would get, because the shiny surface would reflect away heat from the Sun. An ice age would begin.

After initial interest in Croll's work and the recognition of his achievement in developing the astronomical theory, the idea fell from favour. Partly because Croll had the trigger of ice ages wrong, but also because his model was incomplete, his version of the astronomical theory implied that the present interglacial had begun about 80,000 years ago. But the evidence began to mount up showing that the latest ice age actually only ended about 10,000 years ago. Croll's model (which would have predicted the *onset* of severe glaciation 80,000 years ago if he had only thought of the importance of cool summers), slid into obscurity after his death in 1890. If anyone did stumble across the idea in the early part of the twentieth century, it would be regarded as no more than an historical curiosity, not least because the astronomical variations occur on timescales of a few tens of thousands of years up to a hundred thousand years or so, and by the early twentieth century 'everybody knew' that this did not match the geological pattern of ice ages.

Obviously, either the astronomical theory was wrong, or the standard chronology of ice ages was inaccurate. Just about the only person who seems to have taken the second possibility seriously was a Yugoslav astronomer, Milutin Milankovitch, who was botn in 1879 (in what was then Serbia) but who, unlike Croll, followed a conventional route through the academic system, emerging with a PhD from the Vienna Institute of Technology in 1904. Even so, there are similarities between the careers of the two pioneers. Milankovitch worked as an engineer for five years, but always hankered after more cosmic calculations than the design of a building or a bridge. He was, he wrote in his 1936 book *Durch ferne Welten und Zeiten (Through Distant Worlds and Times)* 'on the lookout for a cosmic problem', and in 1909 he took up a post at the University of Belgrade, where he taught physics, mechanics and astronomy. It was a step into the backwoods of European science, but like Croll's janitoring job it left him with time to think for himself. Within two years, he found his cosmic problem – he would devote himself to developing a mathematical theory to describe the changing climate not just of the Earth but of Mars and Venus as well.

The idea was simple. First, he would calculate the amount of heat from the Sun arriving at different latitudes of the Earth in different months today. Then, he would be able to calculate the climatic patterns on distant worlds, without ever having to go to Mars or Venus to measure the temperature. Finally, he could apply the theory to distant times, calculating how the climate of the Earth had varied in the past. But though the idea was simple, its execution was as demanding as the labours of Hercules. There were no electronic computers in the second decade of the twentieth century, and Milankovitch had to work out all his sums using pencil and paper. The calculations were almost endless, and it took him more than 30 years to complete his life's work. He took it with him everywhere, including on holiday, and worked on it every day. We don't intend to retrace every step of that labour of love, but to leap forward and present you with the fully-fledged, modern version of the Milankovitch model, which so neatly fits the pattern of ice age/interglacial fluctuations revealed by the isotope thermometer.

All these variations are caused by the changing gravitational tug on the Earth produced by the Sun, the Moon and the other planets, as each heavenly body follows its own path through space. The way the Earth tilts and wobbles as it orbits around the Sun, and the way in which the orbit itself changes slightly, from more circular to more elliptical and back again, actually produces three associated rhythmic variations in the amount of heat reaching the northern hemisphere in each season (the total amount of heat reaching the entire hemisphere over a whole year is always the same; *all* that changes is the way heat is distributed through the year). One cycle is about 100,000 years long, one checks in at about 40,000 years, and the third is a complicated set of variations around 23,000 years long. Modern computer calculations show how these three varying cycles add together to produce a pattern of variations that closely matches the pattern of roughly 100,000 years of an ice age and 10,000 years of interglacial revealed by the isotope thermometer. Mathematical analysis of the fluctuations in temperature revealed by the isotopes show up exactly the same set of three fundamental rhythms, 100,000, 40,000 and 23,000 years long, beating together. If the Milankovitch model had not already been worked out when this discovery was made, it would have had to have been invented very quickly to account for the discovery. No two ice age/interglacial cycles are exactly the same, but for two million years the real world has marched to the astronomical beat. The Milankovitch model has now become fully accepted as the best explanation of the ice age rhythms.

Although there have been previous ice epochs on Earth, when one or both poles has been covered by land, the ice epoch in which the human line has emerged may be unique. This seems to be the only time that a frozen southern continent has been balanced in the north by a nearly landlocked polar ocean. And the Milankovitch rhythms can exert their influence strongly because the presence of dry land around the north polar region provides a platform on which snow and ice can build when summers are cool. The Milankovitch rhythms may be a unique feature of the current ice epoch, and that explains why another unique feature of our planet today, intelligent life, also emerged during the present ice epoch.

Ice age people

Whatever the exact cause of the ice age rhythms, the important point for our story is that during the Pleistocene (of which the present Holocene Epoch is only a part), the Earth has indeed been plunged into a succession of long ice ages, broken by short interglacials. This has never happened before. Instead of the climate changing slowly and steadily over a very long period of time (while those species that are able adapt to the trend), or changing abruptly into a new pattern (with many species going extinct and the survivors evolving to fill the vacant ecological niches), we have had both effects operating, in miniature, repeatedly. The recent pattern has been one of successive recurrence of harsher conditions, broken by short-lived breathing spaces, times of more equable climate. In the heartland of Africa, where our story is still focused, the harsh conditions showed themselves as dry ages, rather than ice ages, with woodlands dying back and both plants and animals having an intensified struggle for survival. The interglacials correspond to wetter intervals, when trees and other plants temporarily flourished, and animals found life easier. We believe that this repeated tightening of the evolutionary screw and easing off of the pressure hastened the evolution of the human line, by putting cunning and adaptability at a premium, and providing opportunities for an *intelligent* upright ape to succeed in a changing world.

Each time that the forest shrank, the apes that were best adapted to the woodland life would continue to do well, deep in the heartland of the surviving forests. Out on the plains, animals that were adapted to the way of life on the savannah would also do well. The creatures that would suffer most would be the ones that inhabited the edge of the forest, including apes that had not yet entirely abandoned their brachiating past. As the forest shrank, there would be more competition for space in the trees, and the least successful woodland apes would be pushed further out onto the plains. There, they had to survive or die. Many must have died, with only the most cunning individuals surviving. If the dry age had lasted for a million years, maybe all of these reluctant plains dwellers would have been wiped out. But after a hundred thousand years or so, the rains returned and the forests, temporarily, thrived. There was space for the upright apes to recover – both literally, if they retreated to the shelter of the woods, and metaphorically, in the breathing space brought by more plentiful food supplies and reduced ecological pressure. Just as the numbers of their species were beginning to build up again, however, back would come the drought, winnowing out the less adaptable individuals and, once again, putting a premium on intelligence and adaptability. Repeat that cycle a dozen times or more over a couple of million years, with natural selection taking its toll of the dimwitted each time, and is it any wonder that the survivors of the apes that got pushed out of the woods became quite bright?

In each ice (dry) age, many individuals die. While some species respond by becoming better forest apes, or more efficient plains carnivores, only the most intelligent and adaptable individual plains apes survive. They pass on their successful genes to their descendants. In the interglacials, the descendants spread out. The living is easy, and proto-people, selected for adaptability and cunning, do well. But in the next dry age, once again only the most adaptable, the ones who can cope with harsh, changing conditions, do well. If the ice had come in force four million, or even three million, years ago, and stayed, East Africa might have turned into a desert, and all the African apes would have died out. Our ancestors survived, and we are here today, because of the unusual pattern of climatic changes they experienced. We are, indeed, children of the ice.

Homo erectus, driven by these climatic rhythms, spread out of Africa and around most of the world during the Pleistocene. For a million years, the species stayed much the same, apart from a steady growth in brain capacity, indicating the increasing intelligence of the upright ape. But somewhere between about 400,000 and 200,000 years ago there was the beginning of a much bigger increase in brain size, accompanied by a thinning of the skull bones of our ancestors. They had become *Homo sapiens*, modern human beings in all except minor anatomical details. Soon after, the *sapiens* line split. By 100,000 years ago, two sub-species existed, although not necessarily side by side. One, bigger built and with the larger brain, lived in western Europe (south of the ice) and across into the Near East and central Asia. It thrived until about 40,000 years ago, in the midst of the latest ice age, and then disappeared from the fossil scene. It is known as *Homo sapiens neanderthalis*, or Neanderthal Man.

The epithet 'neanderthal' today conjures up for most people an image of a dimwitted, shambling ape-man; but this is an unfortunate misconception and a vicious libel on a very close relation of ours who was both fully upright and intelligent, and thrived in a variety of environments from the edge of the ice cap in Europe to Central Asia. Neanderthals were the first people known to have buried their dead. Their bodies, carefully laid to rest, were sometimes accompanied by valuable flints and stone tools, and food for their journey into the afterlife; at one famous site in the mountains of present day Iraq a man was buried in a grave filled with spring flowers. Neanderthals were not shambling ape-men, but sensitive and caring people who seem to have disappeared from the evolutionary scene because they were overwhelmed by the even greater success of their closest relations, *Homo sapiens sapiens*. The relationship is so close, indeed, that it is possible that the Neanderthals disappeared not by going extinct, but through interbreeding with our own line. It would be nice to think that the genetic line responsible for the flower-filled burial 60,000 years ago in the Zagros Mountains still survives in us today.

Fully modern humans, *Homo sapiens sapiens*, were also around by 100,000 years ago, more or less at the beginning of the latest ice age in the present ice epoch. One likely pattern of the emergence of our own variation on the upright ape theme is that the human form first emerged, as *erectus* had done, in Africa. This is backed up by the discovery of part of a human skull, 115,000 years old, in a cave in South Africa. If this idea is correct, then *Homo sapiens sapiens* probably moved out of Africa in its turn, interbreeding with and replacing other varieties of *Homo* derived from *erectus* stock, including Neanderthals. It may be that there were two main waves of *Homo sapiens*, first the Neanderthals and then ourselves, hot on their heels. Nobody can be sure exactly how we emerged from the *erectus* line. But although we may never know the details of how *Homo sapiens sapiens* finally appeared on the scene, we do know what happened next.

The Neanderthals disappeared about 40,000 years ago in the Near East, and 35,000 years ago in Europe. For the next 25,000 years, while the world was still in the grip of an ice age, it was *sapiens sapiens* alone which represented the *Homo* line. They did well enough even during the last, and among the most severe, stages of that ice age, as fossil remains, carvings and cave paintings from France and Spain, in particular, show. Ice age humans completed the peopling of the world begun, a million years before, by *Homo erectus*. They spread down through Asia to Australia, and north over the land bridge into America, continents that *erectus* never reached. There is some evidence that a gap in the ice between the Laurentide ice sheet and the coastal glaciers west of the Rockies may have allowed humans to begin to move south into first the northern and then the southern American continents about 25,000 years ago. When the ice melted and the Bering Strait became filled with water once again, they would be cut off from their cousins until the arrival of Viking voyagers from Europe about a thousand years ago. How the Vikings got there is a story that involves, as we tell in chapter 6, the growth of civilization in the Middle East and then in Europe as the ice age gave way to an interglacial.

The interglacial itself was no different, except in detail, from the dozen or so interglacials that had preceded it since the time of *Homo habilis*. It just happened that this was the first interglacial after the winnowing process of ice age rhythms had resulted in the appearance of a *very* bright ape on the scene. The first humans had already adapted to every continent of the globe, and the worst weather the ice age could throw at them, and were still doing quite nicely, thank you, when the ice began to retreat. So when the more equable conditions of the interglacial set in, they didn't have to use the breathing space to recover from past deprivations. Instead, they exploded into prominence as the number one species on Earth, creators of the first civilizations, with an insatiable curiosity about everything, including their own origins. From now on, the story we have to tell deals with history, not evolution. But the history (and pre-history) of *Homo sapiens sapiens* has had a part to play in the evolution, and especially the extinction, of many other species.

6

Why Greenland isn't
Green

If the argument, that the rhythmic pattern of ice ages during
the Pleistocene helped to speed the evolution of the human
line, holds water, then you would expect a similar argument
to apply to other species. The 'evolution machine' of Pleistocene
ice age rhythms should have been at work on other species as
well, producing a diversity of mammals to occupy the diverse
ecological niches of the times. That is exactly what we find.
Out of 119 species of mammal that now live in Europe and
Asia, for example, just six were present in the Pliocene. All
the rest have evolved during the Pleistocene Epoch – together
with many other species that thrived during the ice age, but
are now extinct. Even that 119 species represents only a
fraction of the number of mammal species that used to roam
Eurasia. In the earliest part of the Pleistocene, new groups that
emerged in Europe included true elephants, ancestors of the
zebra, and cattle. A little later, forms more clearly adapted to
Arctic conditions appeared, including woolly mammoths,
reindeer, lemmings, musk-ox, woolly rhinoceroses and moose.
The all-time peak of mammalian evolution, in terms of the
number of separate genera of mammals alive on Earth, occurred
around one million years ago.

As well as encouraging the evolution of a broader variety
of mammals than ever before, the Pleistocene ice age rhythms
also encouraged them to spread around the world. When the
ice advanced, high latitude species drifted generally southward,
adapting and evolving to slightly different conditions along the
way; during interglacials, they spread northward, and radiated

into new niches. But this doesn't mean that they retraced exactly the steps of their ancestors. The southward migration might actually have been a bit west of south, for one particular group of animals, to one side of a range of mountains; a hundred thousand years later, descendants of those migrants might be moving north-westward, up the other side of the mountain range. The pulse-beat of climate encouraged the spread of mammals east–west, as well as north–south.

Although the variety of mammals declined slightly after about 1 Myr, even at the height of the latest ice age, some 18,000 years ago, the region close to the ice was inhabited by caribou, mammoth and collared lemming (among other species), while a little further south the mammal population included mastodon, ground sloth, moose, horse, bison, snowshoe hare, musk ox and a variety of small mammals. But about 15,000 years ago, exactly at the time that the latest ice age was giving way to the present interglacial, a wave of extinctions hit many of these species, especially the larger mammals. The extinction peak occurred around 11,000 years ago. Some 39 genera, as many as 70 per cent of the species of large mammal in North America, went extinct at this time, with a smaller, but still large, number of extinctions in Eurasia and Africa. A little later, many smaller mammals and flightless birds disappeared from Pacific islands and from New Zealand.

Apart from the number of species affected, this wave of extinctions unusually (perhaps uniquely) singled out *large* animals. Beavers the size of bears; bison with horns that spread over a full two metres; and ground sloths *six metres* tall. All were thriving members of the ice age community, and all disappeared around 11,000 years ago, along with species of elephants, lions and other familiar mammals that were giants by modern standards.

It is possible that these extinctions could have been related to the changing climate. After all, they did occur just as the Earth was switching from an ice age to an interglacial. But this seems unlikely on two counts. First, such a climatic shift ought to make life easier, not harder, for large mammals. Secondly, nothing like this wave of extinctions occurred at the end of any of the preceding twenty or so glaciations. But there was, of course, a new factor at work at the beginning of the present interglacial. Human beings had spread around the globe by then. The brainy biped must have been an efficient hunter, and larger mammals would be the obvious first victims of his new found skills. At the same time, human activities would have changed the environment in which the large mammals lived – cutting off migration routes for these animals, perhaps, or denying them access to water holes that people wanted for themselves. It would, indeed, be surprising if the explosion of human activity at the beginning of the interglacial had not left its mark on other mammal populations. Perhaps the strongest piece of circumstantial evidence that people were the main cause of these extinctions, however, comes from North America, where the extinctions were most pronounced. There, mammals had been evolving throughout the Pleistocene largely free from human interference. When the peopling of the Americas began, species that had no experience of coping with the brainy biped were swept out of the way in the twinkling of an evolutionary instant.

The peopling of the Americas

No two ice ages are exactly the same. The one during which *Homo sapiens* spread around the world almost began 115,000 years ago (Yr), with a severe spell of cold weather that lasted for several millennia, but had eased by 108,000 Yr. Instead of a full ice age, there was 'only' an interval of ice age cold spanning, as writer Nigel Calder graphically expresses it, a rather greater length of time than that which separates us from the builders of the Egyptian pyramids. About 95,000 years ago, there was another false start to the ice age, lasting for about 7,000 years; but again the climate recovered to something like its present state. Nobody knows exactly why these climatic crises happened – perhaps it had something to do with volcanic activity – but it is interesting that they bracket the emergence of *Homo sapiens sapiens* in the fossil record. Between 80,000 and 70,000 Yr, temperatures fell once more, partially recovered and then plunged again. This time, the cold lasted for more than 50,000 years.

Just as there were downward blips of temperature even during the previous interglacial, so there were millennia of relative warmth even within the latest ice age. The cold bit hard between 70,000 and 60,000 Yr, but slightly less hard from 60,000 to 20,000 Yr. Around 50,000 Yr, there were several millennia of less harsh conditions, and a shorter lived, but even milder, run of centuries around 30,000 Yr. These easings of the climatic screw coincide tantalizingly well with the sudden spread of *Homo sapiens sapiens* and the disappearance of *neanderthalis* from the scene; but there is no way of telling for sure whether climate played a key role in these developments, or simply helped the brainy ape who was by now ready to take over the world. Either way, the ice age still had a trick up its sleeve. The greatest advance of northern ice (the 'last glacial maximum') actually occurred as recently as 18,000 Yr, heralding about 4,000 years of the worst ice age weather, before the thaw began. Some time between about 12,000 Yr and 10,000 Yr, the ice age ended and the present interglacial began. Exactly which date you choose to mark the boundary is rather arbitrary;. it took thousands of years for the ice to melt, and you might reasonably argue either that the ice age ended when the retreat began or that the interglacial began when the retreat finished (on the basis of the Milankovitch cycles, you can even set the boundary date at 15,000 Yr, when the astronomical influences tilted in favour of warm northern summers). For the convenience of having a round number, we prefer to date the beginning of the present interglacial at 10,000 years ago.

Somewhat chauvinistically, geologists also use the end of the latest ice age as the boundary between two epochs, ending the Pleistocene and starting the Holocene (or Recent) where the interglacial begins. There is no physical justification for this. In terms of climate and of the processes operating to shape the Earth, the present interglacial is just one more in the long succession of Pleistocene ice age rhythms. The only difference is that people are now taking notice of those rhythms, and like to mark such an important event (to us) as the beginning of civilization by saying that it occurred at the start of a new geological epoch. But then again, perhaps any geologists around in a million years time will see traces of the extinctions of large mammals in the fossil record from the time of the beginning of our present interglacial, and it will indeed stand out to them as a geological marker. Human beings may have become a factor in the geological equations as the Holocene began – and as we shall see in chapter 8, human beings may now even be affecting the pattern of ice age rhythms. Perhaps identifying the end of the Pleistocene with the emergence of human civilization is not such a bad idea, after all.

A combination of climatic changes and human activities certainly seems the best way to account for the extinctions in North America at the end of the ice age. We should, perhaps, make it clear that by now we are not in any sense talking about 'ape-men' or stupid savages. Cave paintings from 40,000 Yr show a world of sophisticated European hunters and the animals they hunted; a grave site from near present-day Moscow, dated as about 30,000 years old, shows traces of tailored clothing, including trousers, moccasin-type shoes, jackets and hats, all decorated with beads; the bow and arrow had been invented by 20,000 Yr; millstones from 19,000 Yr hint at the beginning of grain cultivation in the Nile Valley. And while these developments were taking place in Europe and the Near East, the relations of those early hunters and agriculturalists began to move into North America, across the dry corridor of the present Bering Strait and south from Alaska, through the glaciers (other people were moving south from Eurasia at about the same time, island-hopping their way to Australia, where the oldest known site of human occupation has a firm date of just under 33,000 Yr). Ice age people were fully human, as intelligent as we are and probably more skillful with their hands through constant practice. They could talk, they had complex societies, and, judging by the evidence from burials, they had religious feelings and ideas. We have achieved more than them, in terms of bending the world to suit ourselves, primarily because we have the benefit of a basis of hundreds of generations of human endeavour behind us – and because we live in the more benevolent conditions of an interglacial. If each of your immediate ancestors had reproduced by the age of 20 (a reasonable figure for any time before the twentieth century), then just a thousand generations separate you from the people who first populated the Americas. The chances are you've stood in queue of people that long at some time in your life, heading for a concert or a sporting event; a three-mile long tailback of cars would contain a thousand frustrated drivers. And just a thousand people, in a line stretching back in time, not space, links you with those American pioneers.

Of course, people didn't just march over the land corridor and head off southward with their packs on their backs. At each stage of the process, most people stayed where they were, and made a living from the land near their settlements. Growing populations, and adventurous spirits, would result in new settlements being established, just over the next hill, or down in the next valley. Nobody *planned* to populate the Americas; it just happened, rather in the way that the first European settlers in the east of the continent, thousands of years later, just naturally drifted westward in the search for peace and quiet, and a bit of land where they could make a living and raise the kids. The trouble was, when the kids grew up they needed some land of their own, and so the migration just had to carry on. The first Americans may have been hunters, rather than farmers, but the same need applied – especially when over-enthusiastic hunting reduced the population of food animals in a locality.

Successive waves of immigrants moved in to Alaska during the relatively mild conditions from about 40,000 Yr onward. The experts still argue about details of the timing of these movements, but several Alaskan sites have yielded bone implements that date back at least 27,000 years. How and when the first adventurers risked the journey south through the corridor between the great glaciers can never be determined, but since the gap in the ice closed during the last glacial maximum 18,000 years ago, it seems certain that only small bands of people can have made the journey before then. Perhaps the descendants of those pioneers lived quietly on the fringes of the ice, following an 'Eskimo' way of life, until the thaw began; perhaps no significant numbers of people moved south from Alaska until after the ice began to melt. Either way, when the ice did melt there were people in the northern part of the Americas who were ready to spread southward as the climate changed. The timing of that spread follows the change in climate so closely that it cannot be a coincidence. Quite suddenly, in a short space of time around 11,000 years ago, people spread across all of North America, leaving traces, in the form of characteristic arrow and spear heads, from the Pacific to the Atlantic, and from Alaska to Mexico.

For such recent archeological remains, the dating becomes very precise. By 10,900 Yr, there were people throughout

Central America, and beginning to move into South America; it took their descendants only another 300 years to reach and pass the line of the Amazon, and by 10,000 Yr even the tip of the continent was occupied. In a thousand years, exactly at the end of the ice age, humans spread from Alaska to Cape Horn – wiping out many species of large mammals along the way. Half a world away, the same climatic changes that led to the peopling of the Americas were encouraging the development of a new way of life, that became known as civilization.

The warmth and the wet

Hardly surprisingly, the warmest part of the present interglacial occurred just after the end of the latest ice age. With the present-day geography of the globe, it takes all the Milankovitch rhythms working together to pull the world out of an ice age and start an interglacial. Once the ice has melted, the rhythms may begin to get out of step with one another, weakening the warming influence. But even if the planet cools off a little as a result, the ice age will not return immediately, because the bare ground and open sea revealed by the retreat of the ice is more efficient at absorbing heat from the Sun than the reflective ice sheets were. So the typical pattern of an interglacial is to start with a burst of warmth, and then to slide slowly but inevitably, with minor ups and downs of temperature, back towards conditions which will allow the ice to advance once again. Each mild spell during the interglacial is less mild than the one before; each cold snap is harder than the last burst of cold, until one day a cold snap starts and doesn't end for a hundred thousand years.

The early Holocene was both warm and wet. It rained a lot, because the increase in temperature meant that there was more evaporation from the oceans (and inland lakes and seas), increasing the amount of water vapour in the air and making more clouds. Increased rainfall meant, among other things, the spread of northern forests over what had been dry grasslands. It was also pretty wet in regions where the ice was melting, a process that didn't happen overnight or in a single year, but which took centuries, even millennia, to complete. And as ice melted and the sea-level rose, it was pretty wet in coastal regions around the globe, with land that had been dry for at least 70,000 years flooding as the sea returned. In the north, the flooding was even worse. Huge areas of Siberia, for example, had literally been pressed down by the weight of ice above, sinking into the treacly layers of molten rock below the surface. When the ice melted, the weight was relieved, but the land could only lift back up to its former height very slowly through the clinging magma – indeed, the process is still going on now, 10,000 years later. So the Arctic Ocean flooded in over the depressed land surface.

At the same time, other areas of water, great inland lakes and both freshwater and salty inland seas, were drying up. During the ice age, partly because of shifts in the wind patterns and rainfall belts, and partly because water from the edge of the ice sheets could evaporate in summer to make clouds and bring rain to regions that are now far from moisture-bearing air streams, there were enormous numbers of lakes south of the ice in regions such as North America and Europe. The Great Salt Lake of Utah is just a remnant of an ice age sea, known as Lake Bonneville, that covered an area of 50,000 square kilometres to a depth of 300 metres – and there were other inland seas about half as big in north-western Nevada and in south-eastern California. The Caspian Sea was twice as big as it is today, spreading into the central and eastern part of modern Russia, and still comparably big even when the ice began to retreat and northern Siberia was flooded. Indeed, the lakes themselves may have *grown* at first, as the ice melted back and there was more moisture in the air.

The effects of all this on human populations were dramatic. The remains they have left behind show that early populations of people preferred to live near the seas. Fish may have been an important part of their diet, and they had, it seems, learned the trick of preserving food with the aid of salt, which they could get from sea water. Ice age people were also seaside people, certainly around the Mediterranean and the North Sea, and along the Great Australian Bight, as well as in other parts of the world. Some researchers suggest that the main centres of these early human populations were in regions that are now submerged beneath the waves; it is argued that the immediate effect of the climatic change and coastal flooding at the end of the ice age may have been to *reduce* the number of human beings in the world, and that the accompanying disasters are the origin of the legends of a great flood that have come down to us from ancient times. From 15,000 Yr to 10,000 Yr, global sea-level rose by at least 50 metres; by 5,000 Yr, it had risen a further 40 metres. Since then, it has never been more than a few metres above or below its present level.

The warmth and wetness of the early Holocene – a time sometimes referred to as the 'postglacial optimum' – were at a peak between about 7,000 and 5,000 years ago. The world was generally about 2°C warmer than in the middle of the twentieth century (perhaps 10°C higher than temperatures had been during the last glacial maximum), and there is virtually no evidence of any major deserts at that time. Rivers flowed in the centre of what is now the Sahara, and other modern desert regions, such as the Thar, or Rajasthan, in India, had twice or three times as much annual rainfall as they have had in recent years. Such changes encouraged the development of human activities around the world, once the shock of the initial postglacial flooding had been overcome.

Into – and out of – the fertile crescent

Archeological evidence from the caves of the Zagros Mountains, which lie across the borders of modern Iran, Iraq, Turkey and Syria, show that people had begun to herd sheep and goats and to cultivate grain by 11,000 years ago. Not far away, at about the same time, the world's first city (we would probably refer to it as a village today) was being built at the site of Jericho, in the Jordan valley and near the Dead Sea. The Dead Sea was one of the great ice age inland seas that was now in retreat, drying up and leaving behind great deposits of salt. This salt was the reason for the city's existence there, a valuable resource used not just for preserving food but in tanning leather and in baking.

Agriculture seems to have developed independently in three main centres around the world. The first, and the one we shall concentrate on most, was in the so-called fertile crescent, sweeping from the eastern Mediterranean region around Jericho and the Zagros Mountains east to the valleys of the Tigris and

Euphrates rivers and down to the head of the Persian Gulf. The second centre of agriculture was in China, where rice, millet and yams (among others) were cultivated, and pigs herded, about 7,000 years ago. And the third centre was in Central America, where people were cultivating crops such as maize by 5,000 years ago. The warmth and the wetness encouraged humans to begin their experiments with the farming way of life. But, almost paradoxically, what may have concentrated their attention on farming *as* a way of life was the retreat of the climate from these so-called optimum conditions.

After about 5,000 Yr, the world cooled slightly, and as usually happens when the world cools, the climate of mid-latitudes became drier. Glaciers advanced in the Alps, for the first time since the ice age had ended; and the Sahara and other great deserts of the present day began to make their appearance. Hubert Lamb, a pioneering British climatologist who has championed the idea of climatic change as an influence on human affairs in historical times, has gathered together evidence for the way these changes affected the people of the time following the postglacial optimum. By 5,000 Yr, elephants and giraffe were becoming rare in Egypt, and by 4,500 Yr they had disappeared altogether from the region, along with rhinoceroses. The annual flooding of the Nile, fed by seasonal rainfall over Ethiopia, reached lower levels than it had in the previous millennium, but at the same time this reliable source of water became increasingly important to people as the rest of the region dried out. Exactly the same processes were at work in the fertile crescent, which in the third millennium before Christ was no longer fully living up to its name. Decreasing rainfall and the spread of desert regions outside the river valleys made the Tigris and Euphrates increasingly important as sources of water and of life. Hunting became less and less reliable as a means of obtaining food, and even the gathering of wild crops could no longer be relied upon. The more the climate deteriorated, the more people had to turn to the relatively new invention of agriculture to support themselves.

The same process, suggests Lamb, was occurring in India and China; and he mentions the proposal made by a Japanese meteorologist, Hideo Suzuki, that refugees from the increasingly arid regions nearby may have become the slaves that made intensive agriculture possible, and whose labour enabled the Egyptian pyramids to be built. Biblical accounts of the wanderings of the Israelites in the wilderness, in a search for a new home, stem from exactly this period of upheaval and mass migrations in the Near and Middle East. People were squeezed into regions such as the fertile crescent by the change in climate, and there they learned to become more efficient farmers than ever before. The seeds of modern civilization had been sown, not by the ice age itself but by a shorter and less severe spell of cold, a mini ice age. The children of the ice had learned their lessons well, and coped more than adequately. As the new farmers learned to cope with the conditions, and civilizations became so well organized that surplus food produced on the farms of fertile land could be transported and used to support people in other places who didn't farm for a living (city dwellers and armies, for example), the squeeze into the fertile crescent rebounded into an outward surge of civilization.

Western Europe became the dominant force in world history as a result of this surge. China became a great civilization first, and remained civilized for the longest continuous span of time. But by and large China, for cultural reasons, kept itself to itself, or at least to its own part of the world. Central and South America developed great civilizations later, but these had no time to spread beyond their home continent before they were overrun by other cultures. It was the Europeans that did the overrunning, having developed the culture that, eventually, took itself to every corner of the globe. And that expansionist tendency was already apparent in the early days.

The colder climate brought with it a change in weather patterns that provided reliable winter rainfall but warm summers in the eastern Mediterranean and along the northern fringe of Africa, even while the deserts were spreading further to the south and east. In the north, although there were no spreading hot deserts, conditions were just as bad as in the arid zone. Glaciers advanced until, a little less than 3,000 years ago, they were as far south as they have ever been during the present interglacial. In North America, there were no glaciers south of the present Canadian border during the postglacial optimum; all of the glaciers on the US Rockies today have formed in the last 3,500 years. But while no stories of those cold days have come down to us from native American legends, Scandinavian storytellers incorporated the story of those icy days of 3,000 years ago in the legend of Ragnarok, the twilight of the gods, when three severe winters followed each other in succession, without a summer in between – the *Fimbulvinter* that heralded the end of the world. The great conflagration that ends the story may, Lamb has suggested, have been as real as the advance of the ice, a folk memory of huge and horrifying forest fires that engulfed the dried-out husks of trees that had been killed by the cold (elements of this story, which we now believe was founded on fact, were borrowed by Wagner for his Ring Cycle).

With all that going on in the north, and the deserts spreading to the south, the place for civilization to develop as it moved out of the fertile crescent just had to be the eastern Mediterranean. Egypt, Greece and Rome all in their turn held centre stage; but it was Rome that first took civilization, if not to every corner of the world then at least to every corner of Europe.

The Romans were lucky. Legend tells us that the city of Rome was founded in 753BC. For 500 years, Rome was a minor city state, in a Mediterranean world dominated by the activities of Greeks, Phoenicians and Carthaginians. It was still relatively cold then, with frosts and snow in Rome itself at least in some years. Beech trees grew near Rome in 300BC. But as Rome began to grow in importance, the climate improved slightly. The beech trees, which prefer cooler conditions, retreated to higher latitudes, and frost and snow in the city itself became a thing of the past. The great spread of Roman culture 'coincided' with an alleviation of climate, a retreat from the severe cold that had been at its worst about 2,500 years ago (around 500BC).

The slight improvement and warming in Europe continued until about AD400, giving the Roman Empire a climate that was distinctly less harsh than the European climate of the middle of the twentieth century. As the empire spread northward, the Romans took grape cultivation with them, introducing vines to England and Germany, to such good effect that by AD300 the province of Britain had become self-sufficient in wine – probably the most tangible image, to anyone who has experienced recent English weather, of the better climate enjoyed by the Romans. But neither the weather nor the Roman Empire were to last. The empire fell and the climate declined again (almost certainly a coincidence of timing; there is no sign of any climatic changes in the first millennium after Christ drastic enough to harm the empire significantly, even if wine production in Britain may have gone into decline). There were to be just two more major changes in climate before the twentieth century began. It was to be during the first of these climatic extremes, a period of warmth known as the little optimum (since it was warmer than today, but cooler and much shorter than the postglacial optimum) that Europeans first began to voyage far afield. Although those early voyages did not result in the establishment of a permanent foothold for European culture on any other continent, they did result in one landmark event, the details of which are, alas, lost to us forever. Some time towards the end of the first millennium after Christ, European adventurers from Scandinavia set foot on the mainland of North America, and met face to face with other members of *Homo sapiens sapiens*, the descendants of an earlier wave of adventurers that had travelled overland into America through Alaska during the ice age. *Homo sapiens sapiens* travelling west around the globe had made contact with *Homo sapiens sapiens* travelling east around the globe, and there were no new lands left that had not felt the tread of the brainy biped. As it happens, vines come into that story, too.

Medieval warmth

Almost as if to prove that the onset of warm weather does not always cause an immediate upsurge in the development of human civilization, the collapse of the Roman Empire in the west (the eastern Empire, Byzantium, survived for many more centuries) was followed by an interval of several centuries in which the world became warmer; but European civilization was in such a sorry state that the period is sometimes referred to as the Dark Ages. In some regions of the globe, in some decades, the warmth may have been almost as great as that of the postglacial optimum; but this little optimum, or medieval warm period, was more patchy, both in space and time. Different regions of the globe were at their warmest at different times, and the warmth seems to have passed some places by altogether. In some places, including parts of the Arctic and low latitudes (near the equator) around the world, the warm interval was more or less unbroken from about AD400 to AD1200. But in Europe and North America, the regions of special relevance to our story, the interval from about AD650 to 850 was quite cool, with some very severe winters – while in China and Japan, these decades were the *only* period of sustained warmth between AD400 to 1200.

In Europe and around the North Atlantic, the best years of the little optimum were from about AD1000 to 1200. There are many historical records that hint at the differences in climate in those days compared with recent decades. In the year 873, for example, plagues of locusts, thriving in the dry heat, reached from Spain to Germany; in the autumn of 1195, they penetrated into what is now Hungary and Austria. But just as Europe had been relatively cool during the decades when China and Japan enjoyed their modest version of the little optimum, when the optimum was at its height in Europe, China and Japan suffered severe cold. Detailed records survive from these times, and they were analysed carefully by the Chinese climatologist Chu Ko-chen in the early 1970s. During the eleventh and twelfth centuries, the climate of China deteriorated so much that the records describe snow falling a full month later in the spring than the latest snows in the twentieth century. Plum trees, that had thrived in the northern part of China during the warmth of the previous few centuries, died out there, while frosts killed lychees in the south of the country. Japanese records of the date on which the cherry blossom bloomed each year show that by the twelfth century spring was two weeks later, on average, than it had been in the middle of the ninth century.

Lamb explains these coincidental – but opposite – shifts in climate on opposite sides of the globe in terms of the bodily movement of the mass of cold air over the Arctic sideways, off the pole. More or less steady winds blow in a roughly circular, zig-zag path from west to east around the polar region (which is why it takes longer to fly from London to New York, against the wind, than from New York to London, with a tail wind). These winds, called the jet stream at high altitudes, where they are steadiest, partially isolate the mass of cold air over the Arctic itself. The circular winds, blowing around the globe, are also known as the circumpolar vortex. Because of the influence of mountain barriers on the path of these winds, and in response to other changes in the circulation system of the world (perhaps linked with changing patterns of sea surface temperatures), the whole vortex and cap of cold polar air can shift across the Arctic region, and may be centred, in any one year or decade, either on the Pacific side of the pole or the Atlantic side. From 1000 to 1200, says Lamb, the vortex must have lain on the Pacific side of the pole. That would have shifted climate zones around the Atlantic northward, and climate zones around the Pacific southward – bringing cold to China, Japan and the whole North Pacific region, but leaving Europe, North America, and the North Atlantic basking in the warmth of the little optimum. Nobody knows why the vortex should have shifted in this way at that time, or even if there was any particular reason for the shift. The vortex, after all, has to be centred *somewhere* in the Arctic region, and maybe it just happened to be over by the Pacific in those centuries. The reasons for this climatic shift are not our concern here; what does concern us is its effect on the human population of Europe, and especially on the Viking voyagers of the Norse lands.

During this peak of the European little optimum, vine cultivation extended up to 5° further north in latitude and 200 metres higher above sea level than in the 1960s, suggesting that average temperatures were a little more than 1°C higher in those days. But climatologists and historians are no longer dependent on such proxy records of climatic change once we move to within a thousand years of the present day. The ice sheets over Greenland, laid down as layers of snow falling each year and accumulating on top of each other, contain frozen in their heart a direct record of the average temperature of the North Atlantic region each year. By drilling into the ice and extracting a long core of these layered ice sediments, which can be dated by counting the layers downward from the surface (rather like dating a piece of wood by counting its rings), climatologists can read this record, a frozen thermometer that reveals how temperatures have changed, if not quite from year to year then certainly from decade to decade.

Apart from the little difficulties inherent in drilling a core of ice 404 metres long, extracting it from the ice sheet, and counting the layers of ice to provide a calendar going back for 1,420 years, the Danish researchers who first obtained such a record of variations in North Atlantic climate since the sixth century had to measure the proportions of different kinds of oxygen atoms in the ice from different layers, in order to take the temperature of the world when that ice was falling as snow. We won't go into details, but trust you will believe us when we tell you that this is not easy. The trick is essentially the same as the technique used to calibrate the Milankovitch rhythms. It depends upon the fact that there are two forms of oxygen, oxygen-18 and oxygen-16, in the air and in the water (H_2O) of our planet. As we have already seen, oxygen-18 is heavier than oxygen-16, so some water molecules are heavier than others. Lighter molecules of water evaporate more easily from the ocean to form clouds and, in the far north, those clouds produce snow. The exact proportion of oxygen-18 that gets into the clouds (and therefore into the snow) depends on the average temperature over the ocean surface in a particular year. So measuring the ratio of oxygen-18 to oxygen-16 in the ice samples reveals, directly, the temperature the year that ice formed from freshly fallen snow.

Temperatures measured in this way can be checked against historical records for the past few decades, corresponding to the top layers of ice, and this shows that the frozen thermometer is indeed a good guide to temperatures of the past. The record shows that in and around Greenland, the little optimum was in full swing by the early part of the eighth century, that temperatures fell for a couple of decades in the middle of the ninth century, and that the warmth then returned and persisted, with only minor fluctuations, until well into the eleventh century. Some more erratic fluctuations in temperature then heralded the onset of a long spell of cold centuries, lasting right up until about a hundred years ago – more of that in chapter 7. But such dry statistics have no way of conveying what the changes in climate meant to people who lived in the region at that time. One of the most fascinating features of the temperature pattern revealed by the measurements of oxygen ratios in the Greenland ice is the way that it meshes in with, and provides new insights into, the limited historical accounts of the spread of Norse culture around the northern rim of the Atlantic during, we now know, the little optimum itself. Cultures in the heartland of western Europe may to some extent have missed the chance to develop during the optimum; but the Viking voyagers made no such mistake, and took full advantage of the opportunities provided.

Westviking

Historians sometimes try to distinguish between the terms 'Viking' and 'Norse'. The Vikings were seafaring adventurers, almost always wild men of the seas, tough and hardy. Some of them were pirates and robbers, who looted, raped and pillaged around the coasts of Europe. They were the more disreputable representatives of the Norse culture, which back home in Scandinavia ran to respectability in the form of 'proper' nations, kings, and the rule of law (if a somewhat harsher form of law than we are used to today). Vikings were often lawbreakers who had been exiled from their homelands. But the distinction quickly becomes blurred. Some of the Viking plunderers settled in the lands they had been raiding, including England, Ireland and a part of France that is known to this day as Normandy (the land of the Norsemen). Some of them became kings and nobles in their own right, rulers, in a more or less lawful fashion, of their own lands. Some even experimented with democracy – the government with some claim to being the oldest continuous democracy (of a sort) in the world is to be found today on the Isle of Man, and is directly descended from the Norse form of Parliament (only 'sort of' democracy because, among other things, women are still excluded from the vote). It was Vikings who had become Normans that invaded and conquered England in 1066 (and their success was in no small measure due to the fact that the English army was exhausted from its efforts at beating off an invasion of northern Norsemen). The people who spearheaded the spread of Norse culture westward across the top of the Atlantic were certainly Vikings. But in a generation or two their descendants became respectable Norse men and women, offering allegiance to the homeland and to the Christian religion, not just to the old northern gods. But the colonies of the Westvikings flourished only as long as the climate permitted.

The Vikings were not the first people to venture into the broad Atlantic. Irish monks were the pioneer Atlantic voyagers, seeking peace and solitude away from the crumbling civilization of the Dark Ages and the hordes of barbarians overrunning Christian lands. Their stories have become distorted and undoubtedly exaggerated in the re-telling down the centuries, but there must be at least a foundation of truth in the story of St Brendan and his travels in the sixth century. Perhaps he reached America, perhaps not; he certainly got close enough to Greenland to meet up with icebergs. When the Vikings established a base on Iceland, in the ninth century, the Irish monks were already there – but they quickly departed, as they found even that lonely outpost of Europe overrun by just the kind of people they wanted to avoid.

The story of the Viking voyages has also been embroidered down the centuries, but large chunks of what seem to be genuine history are included in the sagas, the oral histories of those days that were written down and preserved centuries later. The *Landnam Saga* tells of the first settlement in Iceland, and the *Greenlander Saga* tells of voyages and settlements further west. One of the pieces of evidence that shows how much truth there is in the sagas is the way in which the climatic events they describe match up with the record in the icy thermometer of the Greenland glacier.

Some time in the 850s, on two separate occasions Norse voyagers were blown off course and 'discovered' Iceland, complete with its colony of Irish monks. The monks had eked out a living in a very harsh environment. An early record written down by the monk Dicuil in Ireland in 825 records a visit to Iceland, and says that only a day's journey further north from the home of the Icelandic monks there was a permanently frozen sea. The first attempt at a Norse settlement, led by a farmer, Floki Vilgerdason, in the 860s, found conditions even worse. As we now know from the thermometer in the ice, Floki could scarcely have picked a worse time for his adventure, just at the end of the cold decades that split the little optimum in two in the high North Atlantic. He lost his cattle in a severe winter and, as the *Landnam Saga* records, came home to Scandinavia with tales of 'a fjord filled up by sea ice'. And so, the saga continues, 'he called the country Iceland.' Ironically, that is just about the last mention of sea ice in this connection for 300 years. In the 870s, the North Atlantic was warming up, and other settlers following in Floki's wake found Iceland much more hospitable, and established a thriving colony.

Over the next couple of centuries, in the warmth of the North Atlantic optimum, Norse travellers voyaged to the Mediterranean, trading with Italy and with Arab countries; others moved far into modern Russia, always following the great river systems (the Norse were, indeed, involved in founding the state that became Russia); and some followed the rivers south and east to Byzantium. From 900 to 1100, Europe belonged, if it belonged to anyone at all, to the Norse. And they very nearly established permanent colonies in America, as well.

Floki and the farmers who followed him had not been Vikings in the true sense of the word, although they must have been rather tougher than the average European farmer today. But the next stage in the sagas of the Westvikings fully lives up to the bloodthirsty image invoked by the Viking name. In 960, back in Norway, a rather nasty piece of work called Thorvald Asvaldsson killed a man and was forced to flee to Iceland, taking his family with him. By now, 100 years after Floki's ill-fated voyage, the settlement was well established, and the good land in the south of the island was all occupied. Thorvald had to make do with poor land in the north. But his son, Erik, married into a good family and set himself up on a better farm. He seemed set for a secure life in Iceland when a violent streak to match that of his father surfaced. Outdoing Thorvald, Erik killed two men, and in 982 he was banished from Iceland for three years, to give him time to cool off. The sagas refer to him as 'Erik the Red', and it is tempting to see this as an indication of his violent temper – but it may just be because he had red hair.

Erik, with a shipload of followers, headed west, deciding to use his period of exile to explore a region that he had heard vague stories about, islands to the west of Iceland that had only been seen by lost voyagers who had been more anxious to return home than to explore what they had found. The land he found was, by and large, rough and rugged. But there was a deep fjord on the south-western coast, well protected from the sea, warmed by the Gulf Stream, and with adequate land for farming near the coast. Conditions were rather like those he had left behind in Iceland, and Erik called the new land Greenland.

Just why he chose that name, we may never know. According to one version of the story, it was because from out at sea the Vikings could see sunlight glinting green on the glaciers of the Greenland mountains. A more plausible version, recorded in some of the sagas and certainly fitting what we know of Erik's character, is that he chose the name as a deliberate confidence trick, part of a great real estate swindle to persuade Icelanders to join him in founding a new colony where Erik would be in charge and there would be no threat of further exile. But those written versions of the sagas were recorded centuries later, when the climate of Greenland was even harsher than we know it today, and it must have seemed to the chroniclers that nothing but a swindle could have persuaded anyone to follow Erik west. We now know that Erik arrived in Greenland near the end of a particularly warm part of the little optimum, and that the coastal region where he landed must indeed have been green and fertile, by the standards Icelanders were used to. To be sure, there may have been an element of exaggeration in Erik's sales talk to the people back home – but this was only exaggeration, not an out-and-out lie.

If Greenland and Iceland had been discovered in the same year by the same explorer, then he might, quite logically, have called Greenland 'Iceland', while naming Iceland 'Greenland'. One of the islands is indeed covered by ice, and one is more green and fertile than the other. But they got the wrong names. They got the wrong names largely because of minor climatic fluctuations – Iceland was settled at the end of a cold spell, and Greenland near the end of a warm spell. And that is why Greenland isn't really green, in the agricultural sense, today.

Once they had settled Greenland, it was probably inevitable that the Norse would reach the mainland of North America. Land west of Greenland was discovered as early as 986, by Bjarni Herjolfsson, a merchant whose ship was blown off course on one of the first trips from Iceland to the daughter colony. But Bjarni made no attempt to land in the new country – he was a merchant, not a Viking, short on supplies and with a cargo to deliver to its destination. Indeed, there was so much work to be done building up the settlement in Greenland that it was not until the middle of the 990s that Leif Eriksson (the son of Erik the Red) set off to explore the new territories. Just one settlement, at L'Anse aux Meadows in northern Newfoundland, has been discovered and investigated by archeologists; but that is enough to confirm that Vikings did reach North America at the end of the tenth century. Another settlement, further south, is mentioned in the sagas, which recount tales of Vinland, a wonderful, warm and fertile place where trees bore fruit for the taking, game was plentiful and there was no need to work for a living. The stories, undoubtedly, were exaggerated. But like the naming of Greenland, they must also have had a foundation in truth.

The main resource that the Vikings developed in Vinland, wherever it was, was timber; wood was in desperately short supply in Greenland, and Leif became both rich and famous from his travels in the west, earning the name Leif the Lucky. But while the climate was benign, there was another hazard for settlers on the American mainland to face, which possibly explains why any colonies that were established to the south and west failed to survive. North America, unlike Iceland and Greenland, was already inhabited. Humanity had closed the circle around the world when Viking voyager and native Americans met face to face. At the time William the Conqueror invaded England from Normandy, in 1066, Norse and Americans had already met.

It is tantalizing, but futile, to speculate on how that contact might have developed if communications across the chain of colonies back to Europe had remained unbroken. Would the Europeans have engaged the inhabitants of America in bloody war? Or, more likely in view of the long and difficult chain of communications, would they have established friendly trading relations, leading to the development of an American culture that would be well able to withstand the impact of increasing contact with Europe as ship-building technology improved and direct voyages across the Atlantic became possible? We shall never know. What we do know is that this contact marked the limit of Westviking expansion. Within a few decades, the climate began to deteriorate. The colony in Greenland went into decline and eventually died out. Any

Norse left on the mainland of America had to fend for themselves; their settlements also died out (or perhaps, we would like to think, were absorbed into native American tribes). Even the settlers in Iceland survived only by the skin of their teeth through the worst ravages of what became known as the little ice age. And on the mainland of North America a civilized *native* way of life was destroyed. From now on, the Norse voyagers and their colonies have little part to play in our story. Their tale is very much a might-have-been, and with its end, the focus shifts to western Europe and North America. But we owe it to those pioneers to discuss their fate in just a little more detail – not least because there are important lessons to be learned, even today, from the failure of the Greenland colony.

The return of the ice

When the ice came back to Greenland in full force, the Norse colonies were doomed – not because life in that part of the world became impossible, but because they failed to adapt their lifestyle to the changing conditions. In round terms, the Greenland colonies survived for 500 years, from AD1000 to AD1500, so they were far from being a complete failure. Erik's original colony at the southern tip of Greenland was known, confusingly, as the Eastern Settlement; another colony, further north on the western side of Greenland was known as the Western Settlement. Over a large part of that 500-year span the Norse in the Western Settlement, in particular, were in contact with the Arctic hunters, generally referred to today as 'Eskimo', but in this particular case members of the Inuit people. The lifestyles of the two cultures could hardly have been more different. The Norse were settled people, with farms and cattle, who also used the nearby sea as a resource. The Inuit were nomadic wanderers, who followed their food across the ice and could live anywhere they could find that food, just as they had done since their ancestors moved into America all those thousands of years before, during the latest ice age.

The Norse colonies were small – perhaps 5,000 in the Eastern Settlement and 1,500 in the Western Settlement – but they did well as long as the weather remained benevolent.

Migrating harp seals, that arrived on the west coast of Greenland each spring, were an important source of food, but the summers were warm enough and long enough for grass not only to provide immediate pasture for the cattle but to yield a surplus of hay on which the animals could be fed during the long winters. Polar bear skins and walrus tusks were traded eastward, to Iceland and Scandinavia, in exchange for items the colony could not produce for itself. The most dramatic example of this, and of the temporary wealth of the colony, came in 1125, when the Greenlanders 'traded' a live polar bear for a Norwegian bishop, whom they ensconced in grand style in a stone-built cathedral with its own home farm (by then, the colony was more than half as old as the present United States of America). Two hundred years later, the church owned about two-thirds of the best grazing land on the island (and the colony had then been going for a hundred years *longer* than the USA today). But this very European structure to the Greenlander's society was probably their undoing.

When the North Atlantic cooled in the thirteenth and fourteenth centuries, the Greenland colonies were affected in many adverse ways. As sea ice spread southward, it became more difficult and dangerous for boats to make the voyage from Iceland. At the same time, with the expansion of their hunting zones the Inuit moved southwards, coming into more direct contact (and conflict) with the Norse. And on the farms of Greenland summer was now too short and wet to provide enough hay to see all the cattle through the winter. Even the seals seem to have changed their migratory habits as the climate changed, removing another essential resource from the colonists.

In the face of all this, the Norse carried on their traditional way of life as best they could, for as long as they could. There is almost a sense of epic tragedy in the decline of the colonies. The Greenlander's last bishop died in 1378, and was never replaced; there was no official contact with the colonies at all after 1408, although occasional ships would put in to trade or seek shelter from the weather. Archeological studies show how the surviving members of the shrinking community carried on farming and raising cattle, but the eloquent testimony of skeletons from the graveyard shows that as conditions became harsher and food more scarce the average height of the Greenlanders declined from about 177 cm in Erik's day to about

164 cm by the 1400s. Intermittent contact was maintained with the colonies during the fifteenth century – the last bodies laid to rest in the graveyard, preserved by the frosts of even more severe weather that followed, were dressed in styles from Europe from about 1500. But early in the sixteenth century, the last colonist died. In 1540, ships driven to Greenland by severe weather found nobody left alive, and one dead man, frozen where he had fallen. The last of the Norse Greenland colonists may have missed rescue by only a short time. To put all this in perspective, that last Norseman was closer to us in time than he was to Erik the Red.

But the tragedy need never have happened. The very conditions that killed off the Norse colonists allowed the Inuit to thrive. Thomas McGovern, of Columbia University, New York, has shown how the Norse could have survived, if they had abandoned cattle-keeping and concentrated their activities on developing marine resources – in effect, by adopting and adapting the Inuit lifestyle. Farmers that struggled to the bitter end to keep their herds of cattle alive could have done better simply by changing over to goats and sheep, creatures better able to fend for themselves, and using the extra time this gave them in fishing. An even more radical possibility, says McGovern, is that even in the twelfth or thirteenth centuries the Greenlanders could have developed the kind of whaling, fishing and sealing villages that are characteristic of modern Greenland.

One reason why the Norse followed neither of these options is that they had no wood to build boats. Greenlander boats were traditional, wooden ships like the ones their ancestors had sailed from Norway to Iceland and beyond. Without the wood, they couldn't build new boats, and as the old ones wore out the colony became isolated. And yet the Inuit got around in boats built by a completely different technique, out of skin. Equipped with skin boats, says McGovern, the Norse in Greenland could have spread themselves out in little villages and homesteads along the coast, trading with each other and maintaining communications by sea. The Greenlanders didn't even have enough sense to adopt the warm clothing the Inuit wore to protect themselves from the cold. The stories of frozen bodies dressed in the European style of 1500, and the last lonely Greenlander, may bring a tear to the eye, but it ought to be one of exasperation. European fashions of 1500 simply were not suitable clothes to wear in the Greenland winter of the sixteenth century. 'Single-minded conservatism,' says McGovern, may have been the single most important factor in the Norse extinctions in Greenland (see his contribution to *Climate and History*, edited by T. Wigley, M. Ingram and G. Farmer). You can almost see that last Norseman, muttering to himself, 'If cattle farming was good enough for Erik, then it's certainly good enough for me.'

This really is a most important lesson, since the climate did not stop changing in the sixteenth century. Climatic fluctuations are still occurring today, including some changes in the climate pattern that result from human activities. In many parts of the world, people are even now being faced, for different reasons, with the same choice that faced the Norse in Greenland seven hundred years ago – adapt, or die. The choice is real. Even a 'primitive' culture can indeed adapt to the rigours of a little ice age, as the example of the Mill Creek 'Indians' of North America, contemporaries of the Greenland colonists but who did not make the mistake of single-minded conservatism, shows in the next chapter. Will modern people be less flexible, and less successful, than those long-gone Americans?

7

Of Frozen Milk and Bison Herds

Although the Norse were the people who seem to have taken fullest advantage of the opportunities provided by the little optimum, it would be wrong to leave you with the impression that the benefits by-passed the rest of Europe entirely. The warmth in Europe seems to have continued until about 1300, a little later than in Greenland, and to have coincided with the awakening of the form of European civilization that has continued to the present day. From the middle of the eleventh century onwards, there were increases in population and improvements in agriculture, producing wealth which led to a great phase of cathedral building and to the Crusades, Europe's attempt to wrest control of the Holy Land from Arab hands. William's conquest of England, and the subsequent development of a new kind of English culture, were a minor part of all this activity. But by 1300, or even a little before, this phase of European expansion was at an end.

Lamb has suggested that the beginning of the end of the little optimum may have been responsible for the emergence of the Mongol hordes out of Asia early in the thirteenth century. Just before Genghis Khan and his hordes swept out of Asia, the usually arid heartlands of the continent had, for a time, been relatively moist and productive, as part of the climatic pattern associated with the optimum. Populations increased as a result. The outburst of that population, to penetrate into European Russia on the one hand and as far as Beijing on the other, occurred just when high latitudes began to cool rapidly, and there was a great advance of sea ice southward near Iceland. There could, says Lamb, have been an invasion of cold Arctic air into the heart of Asia as part of this new pattern of climate, reducing the productivity of the land and forcing the people to follow their charismatic leader in a quest for survival.

This, as Lamb acknowledges, is speculation – there is no direct proof that climatic change was an underlying cause of the outburst of the Mongol hordes. But their homeland was close to the region of China where there had been severe cold for some centuries (while the North Atlantic enjoyed its little optimum), and there is good evidence that at the end of the little optimum cold spread gradually westward from China to Europe. Lamb's Genghis Khan scenario exactly fits that picture. That wave of cold does not seem to have been caused simply by a shift of the circumpolar vortex to a new position, but by an expansion of the whole vortex, as well. This eventually brought cold to high latitudes everywhere in the northern hemisphere – a little ice age, that lasted from the middle of the fifteenth century to the middle of the nineteenth century, and which was at its worst in Britain and Europe in the seventeenth century. But as climate declined from the peak of the little optimum and slid into the trough of the little ice age, it was damp and disease, not biting cold, that first set back the growth of western European civilization, in the fourteenth century.

Death and desertion

The setback in the development of European civilization was heralded by an increase in stormy weather. In the thirteenth century, on four separate occasions disastrous sea floods took the lives of at least 100,000 people in Holland and Germany; the worst of these floods killed more than 300,000 people. Between 1240 and 1362, more than half the agricultural land (60 parishes) in the then-Danish diocese of Schleswig was swallowed by the sea; in other coastal regions sand, not water, was the problem, as the strong winds created marching dunes that enveloped many coastal villages and townships, including the port of Harlech, on the west coast of Wales.

Many historians mention bad weather in passing when

describing the events of these centuries, but few acknowledge the possibility that the deterioration in climate played a key role in the deterioration of civilization. In his epic *Hutchinson History of the World*, for example, the Oxford historian J. M. Roberts says that the medieval economy was 'never far from collapse', and that agriculture was 'appallingly inefficient' (p. 550). So when two successive bad harvests in the early fourteenth century reduced the population of Ypres by a tenth, he blames the inefficiency of the infrastructure of society, not the bad weather – seeming to miss the point that in the preceding two centuries, during the little optimum, harvest failures had been rare, and that is why society had thrived and population had increased in spite of the 'appalling inefficiency' of the farmers. No historian could fail to notice, however, that something dramatic happened in Europe in the fourteenth century. As Roberts puts it:

> It is very difficult to generalize but about one thing there is no doubt: a great and cumulative setback occurred in the fourteenth century. There was a sudden rise in mortality, not occurring everywhere at the same time, but notable in many places after a series of bad harvests around about 1320. This started a slow decline of population which suddenly became a disaster with the onset of attacks of epidemic disease which are often called by the name of one of them, the 'Black Death' of 1348–50. (p. 550)

But why did the harvests fail? Because of bad weather. And why did people succumb to the Black Death (another name for bubonic plague)? Because they were weakened by malnutrition. In the late thirteenth century, life expectancy in England was about 48 years; at the end of the fourteenth century, it was less than 40 years. The Black Death was partly to blame, along with other killing epidemics of typhus, smallpox and even influenza (which was still a major killer in the twentieth century; more people died of 'flu in a great European epidemic just after World War I than had been killed on the battlefields of the Great War itself). In some regions, half the population was wiped out by these plagues; over the whole of Europe, the population fell by a quarter. Trouble produced more trouble – searching for scapegoats for the disasters, people often took to hunting witches or persecuting Jews; civil unrest brought uprisings in France in 1358 (the Jacquerie) and in England in 1381 (the Peasants' Revolt). And in many regions the land became depopulated as people deserted the villages and abandoned their fields.

But which came first – death or desertion? Traditional school history books lay the blame for depopulation of rural regions on the wave of plagues. But more recently researchers such as Martin Parry, of the University of Birmingham, have pointed out that the records show that there were many villages with uncultivated land in every part of England in the year 1341, at the time of a great survey known as the *Nonarium Inquisitiones*. Farmland was being abandoned, not just in England but across Europe, *before* the plagues struck. Villages were being deserted before the Black Death did its grisly work on a weakened population, and the villages that were abandoned in the wake of the plague were just those which had been most weakened by the preceding famines, and had already lost two-thirds of their population before the disease set to work. Famine and depopulation *first*, and then the ravages of plague, has now clearly been established as the order in which desertion and death altered the face of rural Europe in the fourteenth century; and before the famine had come the detrimental change in climate.

Scotland suffered even worse than England. The benign climate of the twelfth and thirteenth centuries had allowed agriculture to develop far up the glens, and brought a golden age of civilization in the north, where many English exiles had retreated from the Norman invaders. But in the fourteenth century, crop failures and hunger stimulated clan warfare. In the 1430s, conditions were so bad that bread was made from the bark of trees, since there was no grain; and the civil unrest became so great that in 1436 King James I was murdered while out hunting near Perth. With the king no longer safe in his own lands, the court retreated to the fortified city of Edinburgh, in the south of the country, which became Scotland's capital. In the same decade, further south, the severe weather brought the last recorded evidence of wolves being active in England.

The effects of the climate shift were also felt far away from Europe. In Africa, desert regions became drier and expanded during the fourteenth and fifteenth centuries, while in India various estimates of the total population suggest that a peak of about 250 million was reached in AD1000, and that as the climate deteriorated this fell to 200 million in 1200 (remember that the characteristic little ice age weather drifted westward from China, and therefore hit India sooner than it did Europe) and 170 million in 1400, with a sharper fall down to 130 million by 1550. All this was caused by the development of a stronger, larger circumpolar vortex around the Arctic region, and associated changes in monsoon rains and temperature patterns across the northern hemisphere. Closer to that expanded vortex, in North America, the changes were even more dramatic.

Cowboys and Indians

The Mill Creek people, who lived in the northwest of what is now Iowa, were the local representatives of an Amerindian culture that spread across the Great Plains during the little optimum. From the foothills of the Rockies to Colorado, Nebraska and even further east, between about 900 and 1200 people lived in settled villages in the valleys, growing corn on their farmland and hunting deer in the woods, where oak and cottonwood trees thrived. The period of greatest success of these farmers exactly coincided with the heyday of Viking voyages around the North Atlantic, and it had its roots in the same climatic pattern. With a shrunken circumpolar vortex, displaced towards the Pacific side of the Arctic, the prevailing winds around the Arctic came northward around the Rockies, and were relatively weak. Moist air systems, pushing up from the Gulf of Mexico, could penetrate far to the north, bringing life-giving rain with them.

But when the circumpolar vortex expanded and pushed south, stronger westerly winds at lower latitudes blocked the path of these moist weather systems up from the south. The westerlies themselves contained very little moisture, because they had lost it all in climbing over the Rockies – the plains lie in the 'rain shadow' of the Rockies, and the stronger the westerlies blow the further east that rain shadow extends. All this is clear from modern studies of weather patterns. Occasional months, or years, when the circumpolar vortex expands and the westerlies are strong can be used as analogs for whole centuries of increased vortex activity long ago.

In the 1960s, climatologist Reid Bryson and anthropologist David Baerreis, both of the University of Wisconsin, decided to investigate how such a strengthening of the vortex affected the farmers who lived on the plains a millennium ago. They knew how the climate around the North Atlantic and in Europe had changed after about 1200, and the impact this had had on Norse and European society. But nobody had investigated how and when any associated climatic changes might have affected the contemporary cultures of North America. In the best scientific tradition, Bryson and Baerreis *predicted* that the expansion of the circumpolar vortex and the increasing strength of the westerlies must have made the plains dry out in the shadow of the Rockies, with corn withering in the fields and the forests drying up and disappearing in their turn. Then, they set out to obtain archeological evidence in support of their theory, and to find out how the Mill Creek people had adapted to their changing circumstances.

The Mill Creek region was chosen for their study because it was known to be the site of abandoned villages (shades of Europe in the fourteenth century), which had not been thoroughly excavated previously. When the site was excavated by the Wisconsin team in the 1960s, it provided a wealth of information about the way people had lived there, from 900 to 1400. Accurate dates for remains from different layers below the surface were obtained by a standard technique known as radiocarbon dating, which involves measuring the residual traces of radioactivity in carbon atoms from the remains of once-living plants or animals. The technique became headline news in 1988, when it was used to date the Turin Shroud and proved that it was an artefact less than a thousand years old, and not the burial cloth of Jesus Christ. For Turin Shroud or Mill Creek bones, the technique is the same. Radiocarbon is produced naturally by the interaction of cosmic rays from space with the atmosphere of the Earth, and so it is present in tiny quantities in the air that we breathe and that plants and animals use as a source of carbon. When the plant or animal dies, the amount of radiocarbon in its remains declines steadily in a known way, as the atoms decay. So measuring the amount of radiocarbon present today tells you how long it is since the plant or animal died.

The Mill Creek people ate a lot of game, and left a lot of bones behind. The remains at one site included bones from bison, deer, elk, fish, birds and rodents, as well as other unidentifiable fragments. The Wisconsin researchers looked at the proportions of bones from deer, elk and bison as the centuries passed. Taking just these three species, about AD900 nearly 70 per cent of the bones were those of deer, just over 20 per cent were elk, and only 10 per cent came from bison. Up to 1100, although the proportion of elk bones declined dramatically while the proportion of bison bones rose, there were still more deer bones than bison bones. But after 1100 there were more bison bones than deer, and by 1200 the remains were 70 per cent bison and 30 per cent deer, with just a few elk bones. At the same time, from 1100 onwards the *total* number of bones found at the site declined as the years passed.

The significance of this change is clear. Bison eat grass, and deer browse on trees. A prolonged drought that killed trees would have a severe adverse effect on the number of deer, but as the forests declined and the grass spread there would be more plains for the bison to roam. At the beginning of the dry times, it was easier to find bison than deer, and the changing diet of the Mill Creek people reflected that. As the drought became worse and the plains became more arid, though, even bison became harder and harder to find. But how did the drought affect the corn? Bryson and Baerreis decided to measure corn production by the number of broken pieces of pottery found in different layers of the soil, corresponding to different ages from the past. Pots were needed both to store grain and to cook it, so the number of potsherds is generally accepted as indicating how much grain there was at the time those pots were made. After about 1200, the number of potsherds found at the Mill Creek site drops dramatically. The total number of bones from elk, deer and bison had already started falling even before then, around 1100, just at the time when bison became a more important part of the diet than deer. Together, the various pieces of evidence paint a clear picture – during the twelfth century, the plains began to dry out, and the lifestyle of the Mill Creek people changed as a result. By 1400, there were no more bones, and no more potsherds, being left at the Mill Creek site. The villages, like many other villages in the plains, had been abandoned. But, unlike the Norse in Greenland, the Amerindians had not simply been killed off by the bad weather.

Other evidence from many village sites across the plains supports the broad interpretation of a change in the way of life of the plains dwellers, and analysis of remains of pollen in the soil, for example, confirms that forests died out and were replaced by tall grass prairies. Now this, surely, begins to sound more familiar than our earlier story about Amerindian villagers living in settled communities on the Great Plains, farming corn and hunting deer in the woods like Robin Hood. 'Everybody knows' what the plains Indians were like, from the cowboy movies we all watched as children. Plains Indians were nomads, not settled farmers; hunters who lived in tents and followed the great herds of bison (mistakenly called 'buffalo' in most of those movies) as they roamed across the grassy plains. That, indeed, was the kind of 'Red Indian' culture that was encountered by European pioneers moving west into the plains in the eighteenth century, and the open prairie provided the range land needed for cattle ranching on a large scale, which in turn provided work for the tough cattle-hands of the old west, who became the stereotypical cowboys who shared those movies with the stereotypical Red Indians. Cowboys and Indians, as portrayed in the movies of our childhood, owed their existence to the drying out of the Great Plains as the circumpolar vortex expanded and the world slid into a little ice age.

What has happened in the past can happen again. In the twentieth century, as we shall see, the world warmed again, and the circumpolar vortex contracted. Rain returned to the plains – not in enormous quantities, but enough, with the aid of modern agricultural techniques, to put the soil under the plough and to see corn grown there again, in quantities that the Mill Creek people would never have thought possible. But even in the more benign climate of the twentieth century, there has been only just enough rain, and farming on the Great Plains rests on a knife edge. The dustbowl years of the 1930s, and even the drought of 1988, show what a small fluctuation in climate can do to grain production in the region, which has been so successful in most recent years that it is known as the breadbasket of the world. An underlying theme of Bryson's work has been his concern that the circumpolar vortex might expand once again, bringing prolonged drought back to the region, and ripping the heart out of American farming. But it is possible to fall either way off a knife edge – in the past couple of years other researchers have expressed more concern about another possibility, that the world may now be warming so much that the plains are simply becoming too hot for farming to continue as before, with the grain growing region shifting northward into Canada.

Either way, there is a lesson to be drawn from the way Mill Creek farmers became nomadic Red Indians. Apart from the cold in Greenland, the farmers were faced with exactly the same choice as their Norse counterparts. Farming in settled communities became impossible, but hunting, either on the plains or on the sea and ice, remained a viable way of life. The Norse in Greenland stuck to their farming, and died. The Mill Creek people literally upped sticks and rode off after the game, and survived. Their life*style* ended, but life continued. Whichever way the climate of the world jumps in the twenty-first century – back into a little ice age or on into hothouse warmth – our global society will have to adapt if it is to survive intact. The rigours faced by our ancestors from the sixteenth to the eighteenth centuries, the deepest trough of the little ice age, show just how successfully human society ought to be able to cope even with the worst the weather can do.

When Dick the shepherd blows his nail

We hope you are suitably impressed by our literary allusion. It comes from William Shakespeare's *Love's Labour's Lost*. Shakespeare, who lived in the late sixteenth century in the southern part of England, wrote of a time:

> When icicles hang by the wall,
> And Dick, the shepherd, blows his nail,
> And Tom bears logs into the hall,
> And milk comes frozen home in pail

But why did Shakespeare write of milk coming home frozen in the pail? It wasn't just because it made a good poetic image, nor simply that in Shakespeare's day cowsheds and milking parlours were unheated. The milk froze because winters in Shakespeare's day were significantly colder than the winters we have been used to in the second half of the twentieth century.

The thermometer had not been invented then, and there were no convenient glaciers in southern England where oxygen isotopes could record the temperature. But there was another useful indicator of the severity of sixteenth-century winters, not far from Shakespeare's door. The river Thames provides a marker for severe winters down the centuries. In the worst winters, the river froze into a solid surface thick enough for people to walk on, drive carriages across, and even build tented cities known as Frost Fairs – and all these events are recorded in the history books. The famous old London Bridge, referred to in the nursery rhyme, had been built in 1209, and helped the freezing process. The pillars of the arches of the bridge were so thick that there was more pillar than there was gap in between, and water was effectively dammed upstream, rushing through the arches as if over a weir. Debris, such as tree branches (or chunks of floating ice from upstream), also piled up against the bridge, and in cold weather a sheet of ice would form at this obstruction first, and grow steadily upstream. But the bridge was not the sole cause of those great Thames freezes – in 1269–70 the river froze so far *down*stream that goods had to be sent overland to London from the Channel Ports, instead of coming up the Thames by boat in the usual way. It also froze in 1281–2 and in 1309–10. But the little ice age really began to live up to its name in London in the fifteenth century. Between 1407–8 and 1564–5 the river froze six times. Horses and carts were driven across the frozen river on several occasions, avoiding the toll collectors on the bridge. Henry VIII drove a carriage on the river on at least one occasion, either in 1536–7 or 1537–8, and Queen Elizabeth I used to take a regular daily stroll on the ice in the winter of 1564–5 (this was the first winter after Shakespeare's birth, although he can hardly have remembered much about it!)

In the seventeenth century, the river became an almost regular winter sports attraction. The first recorded Frost Fair was held on the Thames in 1607–8. Booths set up on the ice sold food, beer and wine; there was bowling, shooting and dancing on the ice by way of entertainment. Another Frost Fair was held in 1620–1, and according to legend the sport of skating was introduced to Britain in 1662–3, when King Charles II watched the skaters on the frozen Thames. But the greatest Frost Fair of all was held in the worst winter on record, in 1683–4. This was 470 years after the old London Bridge was built, and it was still standing. Only a little over 300 years separates us from the greatest of Frost Fairs. To the people of 1684, the building of the bridge was ancient history, more remote from them in time than they are from us. But few people in London can have thought much about ancient history that winter.

So many shops and booths appeared on the ice that it was like another city. They were arranged in proper streets, and one enterprising printer made a small fortune by printing peoples' names on slips of paper carrying the legend 'Printed on the Thames'. Even the king (still Charles II) and his family had their names printed when they visited the tent city on the ice between the banks of the Thames.

The ice was 11 inches thick in places, and the river was completely frozen for two months. But the frozen river was not the only marker of severe cold that winter. Where the ground was free from snow cover, in the southwest of England, the soil was frozen to a depth of more than a metre, while the sea itself froze in a coastal band of ice five kilometres wide along the Channel shores of England and France. At the coast of the Netherlands, the ice sheet was more than 30 kilometres across, and no shipping could get through. These were all features of a winter so severe across England (and Europe) that it has left its own mark in literature, forming the basis for the fictional winter blizzards in the novel *Lorna Doone*. A hundred years after Shakespeare's heyday, the cold weather still provided good material for storytellers. Altogether, the river froze ten times in the seventeenth century, and a further ten times between 1708–9 and 1813–14, but it has never frozen since. That is partly because the old bridge was demolished in 1831 (it was, after all, falling down by then, as the nursery rhyme tells us), allowing water to flow more freely; it was partly because industrial pollution and the heat of waste water made it harder to freeze anyway; but it was chiefly because the world got a little warmer after about 1850.

Shakespeare's frozen milk, and the Frost Fairs on the Thames, were as much a part of the little ice age as the emergence of bison hunting as a way of life for plains Indians. The thermometer had been invented by the end of the seventeenth century, and early records indicate that over the decade of the 1690s temperatures in southern England were 1.5°C lower than in the middle of the twentieth century. Between 1650 and 1800 Europe was colder than it has been at any other time since the latest ice age ended – and the cold, though not everywhere quite as severe, embraced the whole world, the first time since the ice age that every region had cooled at the same time. Such a severe deterioration in climate could not fail to leave a mark on society. But there are so many marks, in so many places, that it is difficult to know which ones to single out for mention. Our potted history of the freezing of the Thames, for example, includes a mention of both Elizabeth I and Charles II. In between, in the middle of the seventeenth century and in the worst of the little ice age, England experienced civil war and first the abolition and then the restoration (in a more limited form) of the monarchy. There were many other reasons for the turmoil of the times, and we would not be so foolish as to suggest that privations caused by crop failures and bad weather were the only reasons for the success of Oliver Cromwell's revolution; but it would be equally foolish for historians to ignore the fact that one reason why people were cold, hungry and desperate for political change in the seventeenth century was because the little ice age was at its worst. Other political upheavals, some of which still affect society today, also have their roots in the little ice age. We'll give you a few examples; you can, undoubtedly, find more in the history books for yourselves (indeed, if you are like us then no history book will ever seem quite the same once you know the way in which climate has changed in historical times).

Out of the ice

The cold of the little ice age extended around the world. By the sixteenth century there are good records of the weather from many parts of Europe. The pioneering astronomer Tycho Brahe, for example, kept a weather log in Denmark in the late sixteenth century, and in England diarists such as John Evelyn and naturalists such as Gilbert White kept records in the seventeenth century. Further north, the Arctic sea ice spread southward. In the 1580s, the Denmark Strait, between Iceland and Greenland, was blocked by pack ice in summer on several occasions. In the worst recorded year for pack ice, Iceland itself was completely surrounded throughout 1695, with no ships able to enter or leave the ports; and in 1756 the coast of Iceland was beset by ice for thirty weeks. Just at this time, between 1690 and 1728, there are several reports of lone Eskimos arriving in the Orkney Islands, north of Scotland, in their kayaks; and on at least one occasion an Eskimo paddler reached the mainland, near Aberdeen. Not only had European *Homo sapiens* made the journey across the Atlantic to link up with North American *Homo sapiens*, the spread of the species eastward around the globe, out of Africa and across Asia to the Bering Strait, Canada and the high Arctic had very nearly come full circle.

Scotland, as this evidence implies, cooled even more during the little ice age than regions further south. The sea to the north of the country seems to have been 5°C colder than in the middle of the twentieth century, and there was permanent snow on Scottish mountain peaks in the seventeenth and eighteenth centuries. There were repeated famines and a dramatic depopulation of the country as a result. Many emigrants became mercenary soldiers, fighting in the many wars that troubled Europe at the time (and which themselves had their roots, at least partially, in the deterioration of climate). Many emigrants went to America, in the later part of the little ice age. But the emigration that still has unwelcome repercussions today came in 1612, when King James VI of Scotland (by then also James I of England, and thereby ruler of Ireland) forcibly evicted the Irish from the northern province of Ulster, in Ireland, and relocated Scottish farmers there instead. His motives were partly to increase his influence and build up a power base in Ireland, but also to provide a haven for refugee Scots. In some ways the scheme was a success – by 1691 there were 100,000 Scots in Ulster, with only ten times as many left in Scotland, and more immigrants followed after another wave of cold and famine in the 1690s. But in the long run the move was a disaster – these transplanted Scots were the ancestors of the modern Protestant population of Ulster, and their relocating was a root cause of the troubles that continue in Ireland to the present day.

But for Scotland, this was far from being the end of the tale of climatic woe. Between 1693 and 1700 the harvests failed in seven years out of eight. About half the population died – more, in many places, than had succumbed to the Black Death – and the country was forced by circumstances into a full union with England in 1707, as a means of ensuring aid from the south. It was just as bad on the other side of the North Sea. In the last two decades of the seventeenth century, glaciers overran farmland in Norway and the harvests failed three times in a row on two separate occasions, 1685–7 and 1695–7.

Further afield, in parts of Africa it was flood, not frost, that was the problem. As the circumpolar vortex of air expanded, the rain belts north of the equator were squeezed back southward. That reduced rainfall on the fringes of the Sahara, allowing the desert to expand, but increased rainfall further south and produced great floods in, for example, the region of Timbuktu. Lake Chad, between 13°N and 14°N, was four metres higher in the seventeenth century than it is today, and there were heavy summer rains over Ethiopia, bringing very high floods on the River Nile. In India, however, the expansion of the vortex pushed monsoon rain systems aside on many occasions in the seventeenth century, bringing drought more frequently than in the twentieth century.

North America, by now beginning to be settled by Europeans, also suffered. The winter of 1607–8 was particularly severe, spreading death among both the European and the native populations of Maine, and leaving Lake Superior frozen so hard that around the edges of the lake the ice could still bear the weight of a man as late as June. But the presence of European settlers in North America is a reminder that the little ice age also coincided with a great expansion of European culture and a movement of both people and ideas out of the European heartland. The expansion was very much due to the invention of better ships and improved methods of navigation, and in some ways it was in spite of the severity of the weather, showing how effective even what we would regard as primitive technology can be in combating the climate. But as far as the movement of people was concerned, the European expansion was also in part caused by the climate shift. Scots didn't just settle in Ulster and roam Europe as mercenaries – they also moved, in large numbers, to North America, along with other people seeking a better life in a new land.

Europeans had to move out across the ocean if their culture was to develop and spread. To the south and east, they were hemmed in by the Islamic Ottoman Empire (which had no need of great ocean going ships, since the empire stretched from Spain to India and could be navigated almost entirely overland). To the north and east, Russia provided an equally effective barrier against European expansion. New lands, trade routes, conquest and expansion were only to be found by sea. Columbus crossed the Atlantic in 1492. Within a hundred years, a combination of the availability of new lands and the pressure on poor people in Europe resulting from the growing severity of the little ice age began to make emigration attractive to many. In the seventeenth century, about a quarter of a million British emigrants went to the new world; in the eighteenth century, one and a half million made the trip. Set these figures against England's estimated population of just six million in 1700, and the importance of the new lands in providing a safety net for people who might otherwise have starved in the worst decades of the little ice age is plain. Even with this safety net, there were famines, civil war and a return of plague (in 1665) to trouble England alone, with similar difficulties across Europe; what might have happened to European society if there had been no safety net? There were even 200,000 Germans in North America by 1800, although Germany had no colonies of its own, and well over two million Europeans in all had settled north of the Rio Grande by then. South of the river, only 100,000 Spaniards and Portuguese had left their homelands to settle in America at that time, even though these two great nations (unlike Germany, for instance) had dominated the exploration of the new world in the early decades, and had been (and remained) major sea powers. It is hard to explain, on the face of things, why Germany, with no colonies, had 200,000 emigrants to North America, while Spain and Portugal, great colonial powers both, could muster only 100,000 emigrants to Central and South America between them. But Spain and Portugal, of course, lie further south than England or Germany, and suffered correspondingly less badly during the worst ravages of the little ice age. There was less incentive to emigrate as long as life was still tolerable at home. Their migrants went to rule the colonies; German migrants (and British, French and other more northerly European people) went to work the land themselves and make a home in America.

Ironically, the end of the little ice age brought one of the greatest mass migrations westward from Europe. In 1846, the summer was warm in Europe generally, and wet in Ireland in particular. Conditions were ideal for the spread of the potato blight fungus. Once it got a grip, there were continuous outbreaks for six consecutive years, with the effects on the starving population made worse by an outbreak of typhus. In 1845, the population of Ireland had been eight and a half million; a million died in the famine, and many more emigrated. By 1900, the population was down to about four million, and it has never recovered to the levels reached before the famine. Coincidentally (?) the 1840s were a time of trouble in Europe generally, culminating in 'the year of revolutions', 1848. But that is another story. For our purposes, the Irish potato famine stands as the archetypal example of how climatic events forced mass migrations from Europe – although the kind of climate shifts responsible were different in the 1840s from those of the preceding two or three centuries.

There is no doubting the harshness of the sixteenth and seventeenth centuries. Historians have long puzzled over the underlying causes of a dramatic period of economic inflation that afflicted Europe after about 1500. Prices rose fourfold in a century – not much by some modern standards, but unprecedented at that time. The prices of agricultural produce rose particularly sharply, but wages did not keep pace, and the poor starved. There were rebellions, uprisings and what Roberts calls 'a running disorder' which 'reveal both the incomprehensibility and the severity of what was going on' (p. 59). Why did it happen? Was the population increasing too rapidly for new farming techniques to keep up? Were the difficulties caused by a flood of gold from the new world? Or was it, a point few historians seem to bother to argue, because of the climatic deterioration at that time? We believe that climate played a bigger part than most people have yet acknowledged in the movement of people out of Europe in the past four hundred years or so. Just as people are children of the ice age, so the Europeanization of the world is, at least in part, a product of the little ice age. The corollary of that interpretation of history is that climate may also play a more important part than most people realize in determining the future of human society. But before we move on to that, we'd like to close our account of the little ice age with some examples of the way in which even the last and relatively weak waves of cold coloured the lives of those who lived through them, and have left images that linger in our minds today.

What the Dickens?

Back in the sixteenth century, the beginning of the worst phase of the little ice age helped to create a whole new school of painting. The winter of 1564–5, which we have already mentioned, was the worst since the 1430s. In February 1565, while the winter was at its height, Pieter Bruegel the Elder painted the picture that started a trend. It was called *Hunters in the Snow*, and it depicted just that. Lamb says that this was 'the first time that the landscape itself, albeit in this case an imaginary landscape, has been, at least in essence, the subject of the picture rather than the background to some other interest' (p. 223). Before that harsh winter, in 1563, Bruegel had painted a stereotypical picture of the Nativity of Christ, with three kings offering homage to the infant, the main focus of the scene. After that winter, in 1567, he painted the Nativity again – but this time what we see is a snowscape, a picture of people struggling to cope with harsh weather conditions, in which the presence of the baby Jesus isn't even obvious to the casual observer. In the decades that followed, there were to be many more such scenes portrayed on canvas, by Bruegel and others.

That was at the beginning of the most severe part of the

little ice age. Near the end of that downturn in climate, after a brief amelioration in the late eighteenth century there was more harsh weather in the first decades of the nineteenth century – not as bad as the 1690s, but bad enough for people who had started to get used to something rather better. Fashions changed to match the weather. In the 1790s, the new ladies' fashion from France exposed a large part of the upper body; by 1820, fashionable dress was much more modest, not because of moral objections to the new fashion but because the cold weather made it impractical. One reason for the change in the weather may have been an upsurge in volcanic activity, with several major eruptions around the world. Dust and other pollution from explosive volcanic eruptions penetrates high into the stratosphere, forming a haze which shields the Earth from part of the Sun's heat, sometimes for years after a big eruption. In 1815, one of the most spectacular of all eruptions, at Tambora in the East Indies, threw at least 15 cubic kilometres of material into the upper atmosphere, producing spectacular sunsets around the world and making 1816 so cold that it has gone down in history as 'the year without a summer'.

During the cold decades at the start of the nineteenth century, the greatest of all British painters, J. M. W. Turner, began to depict the spectacular sunset effects which became his trademark. They were based on reality, not simply a product of his imagination. Historical climatologists can even use paintings from different periods to help them reconstruct the changing weather patterns of the past. Pictures of representational outdoor scenes, typically painted in summer in Europe, show an average of 80 per cent cloud cover in the period from 1550 to 1700, between 50 and 75 per cent cover in different decades of the eighteenth century, and about 75 per cent cover in the period when Turner and John Constable were active in England, from about 1790 to 1840. Twentieth-century artists show about 60 per cent cloud cover.

And if Shakespeare's imagery was influenced by the weather of his day, so too was that of Charles Dickens. Dickens was born at the tag end of the last phase of the final cold spell of the little ice age. In the first nine years of his life, between 1812 and 1820, there were six white Christmases in London, either because snow had fallen or because of heavy frost. They made a deep impression on the boy, who grew up to write stories which contain the definitive descriptions of traditional white Christmases in southern England. Even by the time those stories got in to print, however, white Christmases in London were a rarity, and today they are almost entirely a thing of the past. But Dickens gave the Victorians their picture of what Christmas 'ought' to be like, and that picture is still preserved on every Christmas card that has a coach-and-four hastening through the snow, or a robin sitting on a frosty bough. Our Christmas cards owe more to Dickens's boyhood, and the last gasp of the little ice age, than to the climate of the twentieth century – but a milkmaid from Shakespeare's day would have found the scenes familiar. Will the snow and ice return? Or has the little ice age left us for good? The time has come to look at how the activities of the brainy biped, a product of the rhythms of the ice epoch, may now be making snow at Christmas, or any other time of year, a thing of the past; not just in London but everywhere except in Antarctica.

8

Dinosaur Days are Here Again

Climates of the past have influenced the evolution of the upright ape, and affected the way in which human societies have spread around the globe. What does the climate of the future hold in store? Climate is always varying, on many different timescales. We can be certain that, if we take a long enough perspective, then both further ice ages and periods of warmth comparable to the heyday of the dinosaurs lie ahead.

If the ice age rhythms of the past million years persist, then the next ice age is just about due – next century, or next millennium, if not actually tomorrow. Indeed, if the little ice age that froze the Vikings in Greenland, forced the native Americans to give up farming, and froze the milk in Shakespeare's milkmaid's pail had intensified into a full ice age, the pattern would have fitted very neatly in to the astronomical cycles of ice ages. Perhaps the 'next' ice age should have started yesterday. Will the warming that has pulled us out of the little ice age persist? Or is another tightening of the climatic screw to be expected? Which way is the climate likely to jump on the timescale that matters to us, and our children – over the next hundred years or so?

One way to make an educated guess at what might lie in store is to take the actuarial approach, used by insurance companies and by planners responsible for sea defences, reservoirs, and other major works of engineering that are designed to mesh in with the patterns of the weather. We can look back at the recent past to see what extremes of climate have occurred over a reasonable number of centuries, and guess that nothing more extreme will happen over the next hundred years. If we are interested in the next century, then it is a reasonable rule of thumb to look back over the past ten centuries – the past millennium – and guess that there will be no patterns of weather in the twenty-first century that have not already occurred at some time between AD1000 and the present. Other things being equal (assuming that no major shift of climate is underway), that should be a fair guide. But there is always the proviso that major shifts in climate do occur, like the onset of colder weather that brought a halt to the Viking voyages. As we shall see, there are good reasons to believe that a climate jump is in store, and may have begun already. But this change is not part of any of the natural patterns of climatic variation that we have discussed so far, and in order to put it in its proper perspective it is best to look at how the climate of the twenty-first century might have developed, if people had not been around to throw a spanner in the workings of the weather machine.

Cycles that follow the Sun

The most obvious feature of the weather of the past millennium, compared with today, is that by and large it was colder. In any plot of temperature trends since 1000, the twentieth century stands out as a period of sustained warmth. The difference is small. If we look at averages decade by decade, to smooth out the natural year-to-year variability of weather, all the fluctuations in average temperature over the past few hundred years cover a range of only about one degree Celsius. But those small fluctuations were still significant, as our description of historical events of the past millennium should have made clear. Most people who live in temperate latitudes think that a warmer world is a more pleasant place to live (which is why warm periods of the past get names like 'little optimum'), and on that basis an optimist might hope that the warmth of the twentieth century marks a breakout from the cold of the little ice age, and will be sustained. But the actuarial approach to climate forecasting would suggest just the opposite, that we have just lived through a half century or so of unusual warmth, and that statistically speaking we are due for another run of cold decades, returning the weather to the normal pattern of the past millennium. Studies of the way in which climate has changed in the past, and observations of the way the Sun itself has varied from decade to decade and century to century, lend credence to this more gloomy prognosis.

'The little ice age' is a term that means different things to different people, because the cold of the past few hundred years varied in intensity over the centuries. The most naïve view of those patterns of intense cold itself suggests that the warmth of the twentieth century may not last. The little ice age was at its peak intensity in the seventeenth century; then, after a run of decades when the weather was slightly less harsh, it returned in something like its former strength in Dickens's time, in the first half of the nineteenth century. There is a hint, in the rhythms of the little ice age, of a succession of particularly cold intervals, separated by about 180 to 200 years. On that naïve picture alone, the next cold blast ought to be due any time now, since we are already 180 years on from Dickens's boyhood days.

But why should the climate vary in such a regular fashion? What could be producing cyclic variations in the temperature of the globe? The obvious answer is that something happens to the Sun itself, changing the amount of heat which is available to keep our planet warm. At least, the answer seems obvious to some climatologists; many astronomers have long poured scorn on the notion that the Sun might vary, even by the one per cent or so needed to explain these climate rhythms, on a timescale of decades and centuries. Evidence has, however, recently been mounting to suggest that the climatologists were right and the astronomers were wrong.

Two hundred years after the French Revolution, the Royal Society and the Académie des Sciences held their first joint meeting, to discuss the Earth's climate and the variability of the Sun. They investigated the way in which solar variations, most clearly seen in the varying number of dark spots on the surface of the Sun, affect our weather. And they found that there is clear evidence of a roughly 200-year-long cycle of solar activity and climate.

The Sun's activity is measured in terms of sunspot number. Dark spots on the surface of the Sun are clearly visible with the aid of a telescope (used to project the image of the Sun onto a white surface) and have been monitored since Galileo first turned a telescope heavenwards in the early seventeenth century. For most of the past 300 years, the spots have come and gone in a fairly regular cycle, roughly 11 years long, known as the sunspot cycle. Twentieth-century observations, including measurements made by instruments on board satellites, show that when there are more spots on its surface the Sun is more active overall, producing flares and streamers of material that break out into space and create a solar wind of particles streaming out past the planets of the Solar System. There are also solar magnetic changes linked with the sunspot cycle. But, curiously, there were very few spots visible at all during the peak years of the little ice age, in the second half of the seventeenth century.

Partly because of this, the 11-year cycle has only been recorded accurately by astronomers since about 1700. But much longer records of the varying activity of the Sun are stored in the wood of trees, in the form of radioactive atoms of carbon-14. Carbon-14 is produced in the atmosphere by the interaction of particles from deep space, known as cosmic rays, with atoms of nitrogen-14. Some of these radioactive carbon atoms become part of carbon dioxide molecules and are taken up by trees during photosynthesis and stored in the cellulose of their rings. Because the age of these rings can be determined precisely by counting back through the years, and the rate at which radioactive carbon-14 'decays' into other, stable atoms is known, tree rings provide a record of how much carbon-14 was being produced each year in the atmosphere. With the aid of long-lived trees and overlapping segments of preserved dead wood, dendrochronologists have built up a complete tree-ring and carbon-14 record going back 9,000 years, ample to detect variations in carbon-14 production linked with changes in solar activity on timescales of decades and centuries.

The Sun influences carbon-14 production by altering the flow of cosmic rays into the atmosphere of the Earth. When the Sun is *more* active, the solar wind of particles streaming out through the Solar System holds back the cosmic rays, so there is *less* carbon-14 production. The relationship can be checked by comparing the tree-ring record of the past two centuries with the direct observations of sunspots. This confirms that the wiggles in the carbon-14 record mirror the changes in solar activity.

Charles Sonett, of the University of Arizona, Tucson, told the meeting (held at the Royal Society on 15 and 16 February 1989) that this long carbon-14 record is dominated by a cycle about 200 years long. There are also variations corresponding to rhythms 2,300 years long and just under 1,000 years long, together with cycles 80–90 years long and the familiar 11-year sunspot cycle, both of which show up in analysis of the astronomical records of sunspot activity.

The special interest of this discovery for climatologists is that the times during this dominant 200-year cycle when the Sun was relatively quiet seem to correspond with decades of cold on Earth, at least over the past millennium, and also, although the evidence is less complete, before AD1000.

The same 200-year period also shows up in analyses of the widths of tree rings. At intervals of 200 years, there is a tendency for the rings to be much narrower for a span of several decades, showing that the trees experienced some form of stress. This pattern recurs in the decades just before each peak of the 200-year carbon-14 cycle. All of this evidence strongly suggests that on these occasions a change in solar activity first cooled the world into a little ice age, and then led to a buildup of carbon-14 in the atmosphere as cosmic rays penetrated it more easily.

In isolation, this evidence might be taken with a pinch of salt. But quite separate lines of research point to the same conclusion. Zhentao Xu, of the Purple Mountain Observatory in Nanjing, described an analysis of ancient historical records of solar phenomena (such as sunspots) recorded in China, which suggests that there has been a long-term cycle of activity 210 years long over the past 2000 years. And researchers from the Centre de Spectrométrie Nucléaire et de Spectrométrie de Masse, in Orsay, have found that traces of the long-lived radioactive isotope beryllium-10, found in ice cores drilled from Antarctica, show a cyclic variation with a 194-year period. Since beryllium-10 is also produced in the atmosphere by cosmic rays, but settles to the surface of the Earth without being taken up by living organisms, this provides a separate direct measure of changing solar activity.

Taking all that at face value, it ought to be possible to

predict future levels of solar activity, and perhaps short-term trends, by looking at the records from 200 and 400 years ago. At the end of the sixteenth century, the world was sliding into the worst decades of the little ice age, and the Sun was in decline. In the 1790s, the Sun reached a high peak of activity, but this was followed by three cycles of very low activity, and a temporary return of little ice age conditions in the first three decades of the nineteenth century. As we write, solar activity is now building to a high peak. The Sunspot Index Data Center, in Brussels, which monitors solar activity, forecasts that this peak will be reached at the end of 1989 or early in 1990. This gives astronomers and climatologists an ideal opportunity to test the 200-year cycle, checking to see if the pattern of the early nineteenth century repeats in the early twenty-first century, with the Sun becoming quieter and the world becoming cooler.

Unfortunately (not just for them, but for many other people around the globe), the world may continue to warm up, whatever the Sun does over the next half century. The 200-year solar rhythm can only produce a minor climatic ripple on the surface of longer and larger variations, such as the shift from the post-glacial warmth to the cold of the little ice age (or even the shift from ice age to interglacial). And the warming we are now experiencing is likely to overwhelm any cooling influence linked to a decline in solar activity over the next 50 years. The effect of *human* activities on climate is already producing as big a fluctuation as any natural change of the past millennium, and the effect is getting bigger all the time.

Into the greenhouse

Global average temperatures in 1988 were the highest ever recorded. The six warmest years since reliable instrumental records began in the late nineteenth century have been, in descending order of warmth, 1988, 1987, 1983, 1981, 1980 and 1986. The 1980s stand out as the warmest decade on record, and global temperatures have risen by about half a degree Celsius, since the beginning of the twentieth century. The trend of temperatures over the past hundred years is not uniformly upward. The world as a whole cooled slightly from

1850 to 1880, then warmed up until the 1940s. There was a slight cooling into the 1970s, but for more than ten years now the warming has returned, stronger than before. In 1988, the world was 0.34°C warmer than the average for the period from 1950 to 1980, while 1987 was 0.33°C warmer than the 1950–80 average. There is clear evidence that although other factors – such as volcanic dust, or changes in the Sun's output – have caused temporary setbacks, the underlying temperature trend is upward.

The global warming also shows up in the rising sea-level around the world. Once again, there are variations from year to year. But the long-term trend is clear. Since 1900, the sea-level has risen at a rate of ten to twenty centimetres per century. This is partly because small mountain glaciers are in retreat, melting to provide more water, which ultimately runs down to the sea (the great polar ice caps are *not* in retreat, yet, because when the world warms a little more moisture evaporates from the ocean and is available to fall as snow in the polar regions). It is also simply because the sea water has expanded as the world has got warmer.

We don't have to look far to find the reason for this warming trend. It is due to the profligate way in which we have been burning fossil fuel, ever since the industrial revolution in Europe. Coal and oil burnt to provide power for industry, to heat our homes or to drive our cars, is mainly carbon, and when it burns it puts carbon dioxide into the air. Human activities have increased the amount of carbon dioxide in the atmosphere by a quarter since the middle of the nineteenth century, and carbon dioxide is a 'greenhouse' gas, that traps heat from the ground that would otherwise be radiated into space. The more carbon dioxide there is in the atmosphere, the warmer the world will be – and calculations of the warming effect of the actual increase in carbon dioxide over the past century closely match measurements of the actual increase in temperatures world-wide.

So far, the effect has been small. But the buildup of carbon dioxide is now increasing very rapidly (it's one of those exponential curves, that starts off rising slowly, then turns a corner and shoots upward; we are just on the corner today), and many other gases being released by human activities are also greenhouse gases (including the CFCs that are also responsible for the destruction of the ozone layer, and methane that is released in large quantities when tropical forests are burned, and from the paddy fields which provide the rice that is the staple foodstuff for a large fraction of the world's population). Taking all of these gases together, the equivalent of doubling the amount of carbon dioxide present in the atmosphere in 1850 will occur by about 2030, unless drastic measures are taken to halt the buildup in the very near future.

On a timescale of thousands or millions of years, the Earth can adjust to this disturbance. The presence of more carbon dioxide in the air will, for example, increase the rate at which carbonates are deposited, and in time a new equilibrium will be established, as it has been after natural upheavals in the past. But on a timescale that matters to people, a few tens of years, there is no time for these long, slow processes of adjustment to come into play. The buildup of greenhouse gases projected for the year 2030 implies that global mean temperatures will increase by about 4°C, with a much bigger increase at higher latitudes (nearer the poles) than at the equator. This is a much larger change than any natural climate shift that has occurred on a similar timescale. The shift into and out of a little ice age only involves temperature fluctuations of a degree or so, so even if another little ice age is due it will be overwhelmed by the warming trend. A warming by 4°C is on the same scale as the transition from a full ice age to an interglacial – and that takes thousands of years to complete.

Such a warming will change the world dramatically. Climate zones will shift. Overall, there will be more moisture in the air, because higher temperatures will increase evaporation from the oceans. So coastal regions in some parts of the world may become wetter, with increased rainfall. At the same time, the sea-level will be rising, not by ten centimetres a century, but by ten centimetres a *decade*, inundating low-lying regions such as the Nile Delta, Bangladesh, and Florida. But as the temperature rises, the continental heartlands will dry out, and deserts will spread in many parts of the world. The Sahel region of Africa, and Ethiopia, may already have felt the bite of the new climate pattern; southern California and Mediterranean Europe may be the next in line.

The speed and size of these changes are so great that they quite give the lie to our cosy notion that a warmer world would be a better place to live. Compared with what is in store for us over the next half century, a return to the little ice age might be more welcome. The Mediterranean region, from Spain to southern Italy and Greece, will become increasingly arid and desert-like over the next few decades – the extreme heat of the summers of 1987 and 1988 in that part of the world being merely a taste of things to come. Similar problems of desertification will apply to much of the southern United States and to Mexico, while the American Great Plains will become too hot and dry to grow corn even with the aid of modern farming techniques (because the reason for the present global warming, the greenhouse effect, is quite different from the reasons, whatever they were, for the little optimum, there is no likelihood that the rains which made life pleasant for the Mill Creek people will return). The flow of the Colorado River is likely to be halved over the next 50 years, according to current greenhouse projections.

But more warmth, and more evaporation from the sea, also means more storm activity. Storms are driven by the effect of moisture in the air condensing and giving up energy (its latent heat) to drive the wind machine. Hurricanes will become more common, and more severe, as we move into the twenty-first century. So will storms at high latitudes. But some regions of the globe may benefit from the changes that are likely to occur. The US corn and wheat belts could shift northward into Canada, while less severe weather would help the efforts of the Soviet Union to open up new lands in Siberia for agriculture. Other regions, especially the tropics, may notice little change in the weather. When the world warms, the effect is felt more strongly at the poles, because those are the regions where most heat is being lost into space and where the greenhouse effect can have a big impact. In the tropics, where the main influence is heat coming from the Sun, changes will be much smaller. On balance, though, the changes brought about by this new greenhouse effect, a direct result of human activities, seem likely to cause turmoil in the twenty-first century, as many regions struggle to adjust.

One of the key problems, even for regions, like Canada, which might benefit from a doubling of the natural concentration of carbon dioxide, is that the effect doesn't stop there. The world will not simply get to be 4°C warmer in 2030 and stay that way. In the twenty-first century, humankind will still be releasing greenhouse gases, making the planet warmer still. Only when we stop releasing those gases (which might not be until the coal runs out, maybe 200 years from now) will it be possible for a new equilibrium to become established, with average temperatures higher than today but with a new, settled pattern of climate zones. And achieving that equilibrium will take a hundred years or more, from the day when people cease adding to the brew of greenhouse gases in the air.

What would the world be like then? This is not a book about the anthropogenic greenhouse effect,[4] and the problems of the twenty-first century are on too fine a timescale to fit neatly into the broad geological perspective we have been concerned with so far. But we can skip past the turmoil of the twenty-first century to look at what the world might be like in a few hundred years from now, after the climate has adjusted to the impact of all the fossil fuel burnt as a result of human activities. The picture we come up with is strikingly familiar.

Dinosaur days

Remember the dinosaurs? They thrived during an era, the Mesozoic, when the world was, by and large, warmer than it is today. Various pieces of evidence show that tropical conditions existed all the way up to latitude 45° (where we find Minneapolis, Ottawa, Turin, and Vladivostok today in the north; all of Australia lies equatorward of this line in the south). Dinosaurs themselves lived not only in those extended tropical regions but even closer to the poles. But the fact that tropical swamps, and river deltas filled with lush vegetation, existed in some parts of the world up to latitude 45° does not necessarily mean that every square metre of the land surface of the globe between 45°N and 45°S was covered by tropical swamp during the Mesozoic. Robert Bakker, as provocative on this as in his argument (now widely accepted) that dinosaurs were hot-blooded, has gathered together a wealth of evidence which is consistent with a picture of dry continental interiors

---

[4] If you want such a book, this anthropogenic greenhouse effect is described in detail in *Hothouse Earth*, by John Gribbin (Bantam Press).

where creatures like the apatosaurus (brontosaurus) roamed, with the lush vegetation and swampy tropical jungle restricted to low-lying coastal regions, especially river deltas. His picture of the Jurassic world, the period in the middle of the Mesozoic, consists of 'a system of broad, flat floodplains, small rivers, shallow ponds, and occasional deep lakes, all subjected to cycles of killing droughts' (*The Dinosaur Heresies*, p. 118). The big dinosaurs, he says, *avoided* swamps; and he has a much more satisfactory explanation for the structure of their feet than explanations based on the old idea of somnolent giants paddling in the mud.

One of the classic pieces of 'evidence' that dinosaurs enjoyed a semi-aquatic lifestyle comes from the fossil remains of a type of dinosaur known as a duckbill, more than three times as long as a man's height. This fossil is so perfectly preserved that the stony remains still show traces of webs of skin joining the toes of the creature together. What could be more eloquent proof of an aquatic lifestyle than webbed feet? But Bakker has another explanation for the 'webbing'. Camels, he points out, have thick pads, like cushions under their toes, to provide support for their feet and act as shock absorbers as they walk or run across the dry, hard land of arid regions. On a visit to a South African game park, Bakker happened to come across the desiccated corpse of a camel, dried out and mummified in the heat. What had once been cushions under the toes of the living camel had become flattened, dried out bags of skin on the mummy, a perfect imitation of a webbed foot. And that, he says, is why the duckbill fossil seems to have webbed feet – what had once been fat shock absorbers under its feet had taken on the appearance of webbed toes after the creature died and its remains mummified in some hot, dry region.

There is, in fact, a great deal more evidence that creatures like the duckbill (and apatosaurus) were adapted to running over dry plains, not to splashing about in muddy swamps. You can find it summarized in Bakker's book, if you want the details. What matters for our own story is the overall picture he paints, of dry continental interiors with swampy coastal margins and lush river deltas. The swamps and river deltas were, of course, the regions in which carbon dioxide was being taken out of the air in large quantities by living plants, and converted into the carbon-rich material of their leaves, stems and branches. Plant remains, buried in those swamps and squeezed and heated as a result of geological activity over millions of years, became rich deposits of coal, some of which are being mined and burnt today, returning the carbon to the atmosphere as carbon dioxide. Could it possibly be that the world of the dinosaurs was so warm at least partly because there was more carbon dioxide in the air at that time, strengthening the greenhouse effect?

This speculation has been made respectable by the work of Keith Rigby, of the University of Notre Dame. He describes the evidence in his contribution to the second volume of *Dinosaurs Past and Present* (edited by Sylvia Czerkas and Everett Olson; see bibliography). Among other features, studies of the nature of ancient stream beds and the structure of their banks show that, at least in the region that is now Montana, the dinosaurs of the Cretaceous Period lived in an environment with a pronounced dry season, subjected to repeated flash flooding. The evidence confirms that the Cretaceous world was substantially warmer than today, but also shows that 'the dinosaurs were living in a much different environment than the swamps in which we typically see them illustrated' (*Past and Present*, vol II, p. 129).

Just how hot was the world at this time? According to a variety of evidence summarized by Rigby, North America may have been as much as 25°C warmer than it is today, while the equatorial region was only about 5°C warmer than it is today. The pattern is exactly the same as the pattern of greenhouse warming projected by computer calculations of the way the weather is likely to change in the twenty-first century, with higher latitudes warming most. And that pattern may indeed have persisted in the day of the dinosaur for the same reason. We mentioned before how the shifting positions of the continents have altered the climate of the globe over geological time, moving land masses towards or away from the poles, diverting the flow of ocean currents, and either allowing warm water to keep the polar regions ice free or blocking off the flow of warm water and causing the poles to freeze. But this effect can only account for part of the difference between present day climate and the warmth of the Cretaceous. The geography of the globe was not so very different then from the geography today, and experts estimate that the difference could account for a warming of North America of no more than 5°C. The other 20°C of warming is best explained as a result of the greenhouse effect.

That in itself links back to continental drift and geological activity. The extra carbon dioxide in the air during the day of the dinosaur must have come, originally, from volcanoes and from outgassing at cracks in the Earth's surface. Climatic reconstructions suggest that in the Cretaceous there may have been as much as ten times more carbon dioxide in the air than there is today. Carbon dioxide, as well as being a greenhouse gas, is an essential ingredient for plant growth, one of the main ingredients (along with sunlight and water) in the process of photosynthesis. Researchers who study the implications of the present buildup of carbon dioxide in the atmosphere, caused by human activities, talk of a 'carbon dioxide fertilization effect', and suggest that many plants will grow more vigorously as the carbon dioxide concentration increases (unfortunately, this may not be an unmixed blessing for farmers; in many cases, it seems likely that weeds will benefit far more than food crops). A strong carbon dioxide fertilization effect operating in the Cretaceous would very neatly explain the enhanced plant biological activity that took so much carbon out of the air and locked it up in coal deposits at that time.

The overall picture that Rigby paints is of a world very much warmer than today, in which there was more evaporation from the oceans and so more rainfall overall – perhaps 25 per cent more rain each year than today, world-wide. But most of that rain would have fallen not in the plain but on the coastal areas, which became swampy, tropical jungles while the continental interiors became dry and subject to flash-flooding – exactly in line with Bakker's picture. The last of the dinosaurs, says Rigby, lived in an environment very similar to that along the Fitzroy River of western Australia today. Dense, tropical vegetation lines the course of the river itself; but away from the river the land is dry, and the river itself dries up at some times of the year. If this interpretation is correct, then this region of western Australia provides the best guide to the kind of climate North America and Europe can expect as the anthropogenic greenhouse effect takes a grip on the world. But the story also provides some new insights into how and why the dinosaurs went extinct.

According to the paleoclimatic evidence, the average temperature of the globe was about 25°C around 100 million years ago. It declined fairly steadily to about 20°C at 80 Myr, and around 17°C at the time of the death of the dinosaurs, at 65 Myr. Over that same span of time, the number of genera of dinosaurs declined from more than 30 before 80 Myr to about 15 around the time that the Cretaceous came to an end. There is, as we mentioned earlier, a wealth of evidence that environmental changes, and especially a cooling of the globe, had put the dinosaurs in retreat long before the final disaster struck. Although we are impressed by the evidence that there was indeed a final disaster, probably a meteorite impact, that marked the end of the Cretaceous, it seems likely that this event was so effective at putting an end to the day of the dinosaurs because their grip had already been weakened by the progressive cooling of the globe in the late Cretaceous. Some of that cooling was due to the rearrangement of the continents. But just as continental drift alone cannot explain why the world was so warm 100 million years ago, so continental drift alone cannot explain why it then cooled so much. If it was indeed the greenhouse effect that made the world of the dinosaurs so warm, as all the evidence suggests, then clearly it must have been a weakening of the greenhouse effect that made it cool. Probably, the volcanoes became slightly less active at some stage in the geological story, with less carbon dioxide getting in to the atmosphere each year. But for millions of years the lush tropical vegetation of the coastal regions of the hothouse world would have continued to absorb carbon dioxide from the air and lay it down as coal. By the time this biological activity had reduced the carbon dioxide content of the atmosphere so much that the world was becoming noticeably cooler, the end of the day of the dinosaur was in sight. A new climatic balance would ultimately be struck, one which would turn out to favour mammals, not dinosaurs.

Our story has come full circle. We are the children of the ice, and we owe our existence to the climatic changes that brought about the demise of the dinosaurs. Those climatic changes were closely linked to biological activity, taking carbon dioxide out of the air and storing it as coal, and so weakening the greenhouse effect and cooling the globe. Now, however, human activities are reversing the trend. We are busily taking carbon, in the form of coal, out of the ground, and burning it to make carbon dioxide, which is building up in the atmosphere and warming our planet. We are restoring the kind of climate that suited the dinosaurs so well, conditions in which our ancestors were reduced to running about in the undergrowth, surviving in the shadow of the dinosaurs. Dinosaur days are, indeed, here again. The whole pattern of climate and evolution over the past 65 million years – the unusual climatic circumstances that brought about our own existence – may be seen, in the long story of the Earth itself, as no more than a temporary aberration caused by too much carbon being taken out of circulation for a time. Although the dinosaurs themselves are no longer around to benefit from the change back to 'normal' weather conditions on Earth, if those hotter conditions persist they could well leave a mark in the geological record as significant as the Cretaceous–Tertiary boundary itself. Time for us to take our leave – with just a passing curiosity about what paleontologists 65 million years from now, if there are any, will make of this new blip in the geological record.

Appendix

Cycles of Ice

We believe that a key element in the emergence of intelligent, upright apes on Earth has been the pattern of ice age cycles that has persisted over the past million years or more. The relevance of these cycles to our story is spelled out in chapter 5; but in order to avoid breaking up the flow of the story, we left out many of the astronomical details from that discussion. For those who want to know a little more about the ice age cycles, which are so central to the main theme of this book, and the way in which the living systems of our planet may be responsible for amplifying the ice age rhythms, we include here the text of an article by John Gribbin from the May 1989 issue of the magazine *l'Astronomia*.

The story begins, appropriately enough, in the century when the little ice age was at its peak intensity, with Johannes Kepler, the seventeenth-century astronomer who first realized that the orbits of the planets around the Sun are ellipses, not circles. He also discovered that each planet traces its orbit faster when it is moving closest to the Sun (at perihelion) and slower at the end of its orbit furthest from the Sun (aphelion). This led to the first astronomical theory of climatic changes – a theory of ice ages. As it happens, that first idea was wrong; but it paved the way for later research which has now established, beyond reasonable doubt, that the rhythms of the retreat and advance of great glaciers on Earth are indeed intimately linked with astronomical changes – with the way our planet tilts and wobbles in its orbit around the Sun.

Kepler's discovery of the variable motion of the planets was important in its own right. It was one of the bedrocks upon which Isaac Newton founded his theory of gravity. But that is not the story I have to tell here. The story of ice age rhythms begins with Joseph Adhémar, a French mathematician, in the 1840s.

Because of the variable speed of the Earth in its orbit, one half of that orbit is traversed more slowly than the other half. In terms of Northern Hemisphere seasons, the half of the orbit centred on the summer solstice, when the North Pole is tilted towards the Sun, is travelled more slowly than the half of the orbit corresponding to autumn and winter. As a result, spring and summer in the Northern Hemisphere contain seven more days, astronomically speaking, than winter and autumn. In the Southern Hemisphere, the opposite applies, and winter is longer than summer. Adhémar reasoned that this might explain why Antarctica is in the grip of ice today, while the Northern Hemisphere enjoys the relatively balmy conditions of what climatologists call an interglacial – a warm interval between full ice ages.

Because of the influence of astronomical forces on the Earth, including the gravitational pull on the Sun and the Moon, the spinning Earth wobbles, like a spinning top. An imaginary line joining the South Pole to the North Pole is not perpendicular to a line joining the centre of the Earth to the Sun (the plane of the ecliptic), but is tilted at 23.4°. This tilt is what gives us the rhythm of the seasons. On a much longer timescale, as the Earth wobbles the direction of this tilt changes, tracing out a circle on the sky. The effect is called the precession of the equinoxes, and it completes the circle in a time a little over 20,000 years long. It is the reason why the Ancient Egyptians, for example, saw a different 'pole star' from the one we use today. In Adhémar's day, it seemed reasonable to suppose that something over 10,000 years ago, when the South Pole tilted towards the Sun during the slow half of the Earth's orbit, there would have been less ice in Antarctica while Europe and America suffered in the grip of a full ice age. But in 1852 Alexander von Humboldt, the German scientist famous for identifying the ocean current that bears his name, pointed out the fatal flaw in this argument. Although the Northern Hemisphere summer half of the Earth's orbit is seven days longer than the winter half at present, this is because the Earth is further away from the Sun in summer. Because it is further away, it receives less heat. Averaging over the whole of spring–summer and the whole of autumn–winter the two effects cancel out – the total amount of heat received by each hemisphere in each half of the orbit is identical.

So, why *does* the climate of the Earth vary, from ice age to interglacial and back again? Adhémar's suggestion proved of lasting importance not because it was right, but because it started people thinking about how changes in the Earth's orbital geometry might indeed cause the ebb and flow of great Northern Hemisphere ice ages. It took more than a century for this to lead to an established theory of the cycles of ice, a theory now exactly matched up with observations, in the form of a well-understood geological record of the way the temperature of the Earth has varied over the past two million years.

After Adhémar's false move was corrected, the first steps down what turned out to be the right path to an astronomical explanation of ice age cycles were taken by a Scot, James Croll, in the 1860s. Croll's story is often told in tones of wonder at the ability of an unsung genius – he was a janitor at the Andersonian Museum in Glasgow when he published his theory of the cycles of ice. But this popular, and appealing, story is more than a little misleading. Although he came from a poor family, Croll had always taken an interest in science, reading any books he could lay his hands on. Family circumstances did not permit him to study at university, and he had to take a succession of jobs (millwright, carpenter, shopkeeper and even insurance salesman), but he always devoted more of his attention to academic studies than to his supposed 'real' work. He took the job of janitor for the same reason that Albert Einstein later took the job of patent office clerk – the work was easy (if poorly paid) and provided him with a quiet, warm place in which to read and think.

From his cosy niche in the museum, Croll began to publish scientific papers in the 1860s, and turned his attention to the mystery of ice ages, one of the big debating points in science at the time. Croll's theory also started out from the fact that the Earth is tilted with respect to the Sun, and the knowledge that this tilt varies as the millennia pass. But he brought into play another important factor. Because of the complex interplay of gravitational forces between the planets of the Solar System, the shape of the Earth's orbit changes in a regular and predictable way. The orbit is always an ellipse, but sometimes the ellipse is almost a perfect circle, and sometimes it is more elongated. These changes in the eccentricity of the orbit had been calculated by the French astronomer Urbain Leverrier (who, like Croll and all scientists of their time, had no electronic computers to assist him, but had to carry out all his calculations 'by hand'). Croll used Leverrier's work as a platform on which to build his own theory.

As the orbit of the Earth gradually shifts from more circular (low eccentricity) to more elliptical (high eccentricity) it follows a cycle roughly 100,000 years long. At present, the orbit is nearly circular (eccentricity close to zero); a few score thousand years ago it was relatively elongated (eccentricity about 6 per cent). So Croll argued that a circular orbit corresponds to the relative warmth of an interglacial, while an elliptical orbit is associated with the cold of a full ice age.

But how could the effect work? Even though the shape of the Earth's orbit changes, Leverrier and Croll were well aware that the total amount of heat received by the Earth from the Sun over a full year is always the same. Croll guessed that what mattered was the balance of heat between the summer and winter seasons. He argued that when winters are cold, snow can accumulate more easily, and once it does so it will reflect away incoming solar radiation and keep the Earth cold even in summer – he may well have been the first person to incorporate this idea of positive feedback into any scientific theory. Thus, he reasoned, if the Earth is far from the Sun during Northern Hemisphere winters there should be an ice age.

This theory conflicted with no known geological evidence of the time, although some scientists were sceptical about how such a small change in the eccentricity of the Earth's orbit – over a range of a few per cent – could produce such a large effect. Debate about Croll's theory continued until the end of the nineteenth century, but by then it was faced with mounting geological evidence that the most recent ice age had ended not scores of thousands of years ago, but only 10,000 years ago. In other words, the Earth was still in the grip of ice when the orbit was very nearly circular. It seemed the astronomical theory of ice ages was dead. But then, in the twentieth century, it was revived by a combination of still-better calculations of the details of the astronomical influences, and, in the past 20 years, comparably accurate measurements of the ebb and flow of the great ice sheets over the past few hundred thousand years. The person who breathed life into the corpse of Croll's theory was a Yugoslav astronomer, Milutin Milankovitch. In his honour, the astronomical theory is now also known as the Milankovitch Model of ice ages.

Milankovitch added one other astronomical influence to the two factors considered by Croll. As well as the precession of the equinoxes and the variation of the orbital eccentricity, the angle of the Earth's tilt itself changes, nodding up and down over a range from 21.8° (more nearly upright) to 24.4° (most tilted) over a cycle 41,000 years long. The present tilt, a little over 23.4°, is roughly halfway between the two extreme possibilities. For the past 10,000 years, the tilt has been decreasing. Since it is the tilt of the Earth that produces the cycle of the seasons, this means that the differences between the seasons are less extreme than they were 10,000 years ago – other things being equal, summers are a little cooler, and winters a little warmer, than they were then (although the total heat received by the Earth from the Sun over a full year is, once again, exactly the same in both cases).

Clearly, this tilt cycle must also have a strong influence on any climate rhythms that respond to the variation in the precession of the equinoxes. But this completes the tally of effects which change the orbital geometry of the Earth and alter the balance of heat between the seasons. By combining all three effects, it is possible to calculate the amount of solar heat (insolation) arriving at any latitude of the Earth in each season at any time in the past (or the future). The calculations are *possible* – but in Milankovitch's day they were an enormous task, still before the era of electronic computers. With heroic dedication, he calculated the appropriate heat curves for a range of latitudes from 5°N to 75°N, and published the results in 1930.

At that time, these calculations were far more detailed and accurate than the knowledge geologists had of the actual way in which temperatures on Earth had changed. Nobody knew whether Milankovitch's calculations matched the real world.

But he also made a key contribution to the theory of how these insolation changes might affect the climate. Borrowing a suggestion from the German geologist Wladimir Köppen, Milankovitch proposed that the key to ice ages is the occurrence of cool summers, *not* very cold winters. The argument, taken up today as a cornerstone of the modern theory of ice ages, is that winter is always cold enough for snow to fall and to lay on the ground. Today, however, the snow melts in the spring. The way to spread ice sheets across the land of the Northern Hemisphere is to have cold springs, and cool summers, so that there is very little melting, and the winter snowfall more than makes up for any summer loss. As for Antarctica, that frozen continent seems to be permanently in the grip of ice; so the average temperature of the whole globe depends on the march and retreat of northern ice sheets.

This, of course, turns Croll's idea on its head, and makes the astronomical theory fit the recent pattern of ice ages. Some 10,000 years ago, when there was less difference between the seasons and summer was cooler, the Northern Hemisphere was indeed in the grip of the latest great ice age. Nearly half a century was to pass, however, before the definitive proof that Milankovitch had been on the right track came in.

Many people have been involved in synthesizing the modern version of the astronomical theory of ice ages. A key contribution has come from André Berger, a Belgian, who has produced the best and most detailed calculations of the varying insolation at different latitudes – this time, *with* the aid of electronic computers! George Kukla, a Czech now resident in the United States, has studied the way in which changes in insolation at different seasons are likely to affect snow cover. He concludes that, given the present-day geography of the Earth, with land at high latitudes in the Northern Hemisphere (something which has not been the case, of course, during most of the history of our planet), the natural state for the world to be in is an ice age. It is only when the orbital cycles conspire to provide the maximum summer warmth that the ice temporarily retreats, and the world enters an interglacial state.

But the most important new developments come from studies of how temperatures have actually varied in the past. The measurements depend on scientists being able to obtain a supply of raw material untouched by the ravages of geological processes for hundreds of thousands of years, and on their being able to interpret this material as a thermometer. They use long cores of sediments drilled from the bed of the ocean, where it lays undisturbed for millennia. A great deal of this sedimentary material is made up of the shells of dead sea-creatures, the microscopic planktonic foraminifera, which in the fullness of geological time will produce new deposits of chalk.

As the sediments pile up with younger deposits near the surface and older deposits buried more deeply, they can be dated by various techniques. These include measurements of radioactive isotopes in the remains, and traces of 'fossil' magnetism. Then, the temperature of the ocean those long-dead sea creatures lived in can be determined, by measuring, for example, the abundances of different isotopes of oxygen in their chalky remains.

The carbonate material contains two isotopes of oxygen, oxygen-16 and oxygen-18, as does every other sample of oxygen on Earth, including the air that we breathe. Oxygen-18 is heavier than oxygen-16. The carbonate in the shells of sea creatures is built up from molecules of carbon dioxide, and these were absorbed by the living foraminifera at different rates depending on which isotope of oxygen they contain, and on the temperature. The proportion of each isotope available to creatures living in the sea depends on the temperature of the sea water, and many studies have established a precise relationship – a geological thermometer – which makes it possible to deduce past temperatures from oxygen isotope measurements. Carbonates from creatures that lived in colder water have a higher proportion of the heavier isotope.

In 1976, two American researchers, Jim Hays and John Imbrie, joined forces with a Briton, Nick Shackleton, in what was then the most complete and detailed study of this kind. They had a length of core 15 metres long, spanning an interval of 450,000 years. Taking samples every 10 cm throughout its length meant that they were measuring temperatures on Earth at 3,000 year intervals. When they analysed the pattern of those temperature variations, they found that the rhythms were dominated by cycles 100,000, 41,000 and 22,000 years long – exactly the cycles studied by Milankovitch and calculated in great detail by his modern counterpart, Berger. Since 1976, these studies have been repeated in more detail on longer cores, and always the picture is the same. Astronomical influences do control the ice age cycles. But until recently one puzzle still remained – how could such small changes in seasonal heating produce such large variations in climate, from ice age to interglacial and back again? The answer has come in the past few years, from another kind of drilling – this time, in the polar ice.

Polar ice sheets also provide a 'fossilized' record of past environmental changes, including temperatures. Like deep sea sediments, the older layers are buried more deeply, and contain isotopes of oxygen, and other tracers, in the proportions appropriate to the conditions at the time they were laid down, as snow. Even the deepest ice layers are not so old as the oldest sediments studied by Hays and his colleagues. But, unlike deep sea sediments, ice cores actually preserve samples of ancient air, trapped as bubbles in the ice.

The deepest ice core of this type comes from the Vostok site, in the heart of Antarctica. It is more than 2 kilometres long, and covers a span of 160,000 years, just over one complete long Milankovitch cycle; it provides a detailed record of both temperature and, from the trapped bubbles, the composition of the air in past millennia. The most dramatic discovery from this analysis is that during the ice age which ended some 10,000 years ago, the concentration of carbon dioxide in the air was only about 200 parts per million (ppm). At the time the ice age ended and the interglacial began, the amount of carbon dioxide in the air increased to about 270 ppm, where it stayed until the twentieth century. Human activities (burning coal and oil and cutting down forests) have now pushed the concentration up to 350 ppm. The Vostok ice core is just long enough to show that the same thing happened at the end of the previous ice age – 155 thousand years ago, the world suddenly warmed into an interglacial state, just at a time when the carbon dioxide concentration of the atmosphere increased from below 200 ppm to nearly 300 ppm.

Today, we hear a lot about the problems that might be posed by increasing concentrations of carbon dioxide, because it contributes to the 'greenhouse effect'. Carbon dioxide allows solar energy to pass through to the ground, but traps infrared heat that would otherwise escape from the surface of the Earth into space. It makes the world warmer. And now it is clear that both temperature *and* carbon dioxide concentrations march in step with the Milankovitch cycles – the Vostok core shows clearly the 22,000 year rhythm in the carbon dioxide and temperature fluctuations.

At one level, this solves the problem of how the astronomical cycles can have such a big effect on climate. Clearly, the rhythms are being amplified by the carbon dioxide, strengthening or weakening the greenhouse effect in line with the Milankovitch cycles, in a feedback process which would surely have delighted Croll himself. The question now becomes, why do the astronomical cycles affect the amount of carbon dioxide in the atmosphere? That question is only just beginning to be answered. At this point, we move out of the realms of astronomy and into biology. The answer seems to lie in the biological productivity of the oceans, the activity of those millions of plankton that are the primary food source of all oceanic life – and which are also, by a nice twist of irony, the source of our information about past temperatures. When the oceans are more productive, more carbon dioxide is drawn out of the air and, eventually, deposited in sediments on the sea-floor. A colder Earth, the argument runs, is a more productive one, at least as far as the oceans are concerned. Nobody has yet explained in detail how this process might occur, but one particularly intriguing suggestion has come from John Martin and Steve Fitzwater, in the United States.

They have been studying the way in which plankton in the north-eastern Pacific grow, and they have found that these tiny creatures multiply dramatically, in a 'bloom', if they are provided with extra iron. It seems that they have everything else they need in the sub-Arctic Pacific, but not enough iron for fully efficient metabolism. During an ice age, the world is not only colder, but also drier, because water is locked up in ice. Dry winds blow across the continents, and carry a burden of dust out into the oceans. One of the things that dust contains is iron. So, say Martin and Fitzwater, as the Earth begins to cool iron-bearing dust is blown over the oceans, where it is taken up by the plankton and used to drive their biological processes more effectively. They act as a 'biological pump' taking carbon dioxide out of the atmosphere, and encouraging the cooling trend. At the end of an ice age, as the world begins to warm and moisture returns to the land at high latitudes, the dust supply is cut off and the process operates in reverse.

The biological side of the story has yet to be worked out in detail, but ideas such as this show that, at least, the possibility of such a biological pump does exit. The astronomical side of the story, though, is essentially complete, with the proof from deep sea sediments and ice cores that the cycles of ice on Earth are the same as the astronomical cycles studied by Milankovitch. Even without knowing details of the biological interactions, that provides us with a chilly forecast. Interglacials last for only about 10,000 years, on average. The present interglacial began 10,000 years ago, when the Earth's tilt was at its greatest, emphasizing the difference between the seasons; the tilt is now halfway to its other extreme, and decreasing. If the pattern of the past is to be repeated, the next ice age is due any millennium now.

Bibliography

Sources mentioned in the text, and other relevant books, are detailed here. Those marked with an asterisk are less of an easy read than the others, but will repay the extra effort involved in getting to grips with them. Editions referred to are simply the ones that came to hand while we were writing this book.

Robert Bakker, *The Dinosaur Heresies,* London, Longman, 1987
Our favourite dinosaur book. The inside story of Bakker's now not-so-heretical idea that many dinosaurs were hot blooded.
Reid Bryson and Thomas Murray, *Climates of Hunger,* Madison, University of Wisconsin Press, 1977
A short, readable overview of the impact of climatic change on many human societies, focusing especially on the North Atlantic Viking colonies and the troubles experienced by the native American cultures over the past thousand years or so. Bryson is one of the world's leading climatologists; Murray is a professional writer. The combination works well.
Nigel Calder, *Timescale,* London, Chatto & Windus, 1984
The best single-volume chronology of everything important to human evolution, starting with the birth of the Universe in a big bang between 10 billion and 15 billion years ago. Calder tends to invoke cosmic impacts to explain just about every extinction in the fossil record, and this enthusiasm for cosmic catastrophe may not be fully justified. But overall the book absolutely justifies its subtitle, 'an atlas of the fourth dimension'.
Preston Cloud, *Oasis in Space,* New York, Norton, 1988
A history of the Earth, mainly from a geological perspective but with some insight into the evolution of life.

James Croll, *Climate and Time*, New York, Appleton, 1875
Early history of the astronomical theory of ice ages, from the pioneer of the subject. Interesting, but not essential reading since Croll's story is summarized very well by John and Katherine Imbrie (see below).

*Sylvia Czerkas and Everett Olson (eds), *Dinosaurs Past and Present*, Seattle and London, Natural History Museum of Los Angeles/ University of Washington Press, two vols, 1988
The asterisk refers to the text, and the books are a little pricey for the lay person, but we recommend them chiefly for the astonishing paintings and drawings, scrupulously accurate scientific reconstructions of how dinosaurs must have looked. Dale Russell's 'dinosauroid' features in volume one. Bully your local library into buying them.

Richard Dawkins, *The Blind Watchmaker*, London, Penguin, 1988
The best book about evolution for the general reader.

David Dinely, *Earth's Voyage Through Time*, London, Granada, 1974
Primarily a history of the changing face of the 'solid' Earth, but with major events in the development of life put in their broad environmental context.

Niles Eldredge, *Life Pulse*, New York, Facts on File Publications, 1987
A very readable account of bits of the fossil record that interest Eldredge, and that he has studied himself.

John Gribbin, *In Search of the Double Helix*, New York, Bantam, 1987
Darwin, DNA and the basics of evolution by natural selection.

John Gribbin, *The Hole in the Sky*, New York, Bantam, 1988
Just in case you *don't* know about CFCs! (See chapter 1)

John Gribbin, *Hothouse Earth*, London, Bantam Press, 1990
More about the greenhouse effect (see chapter 8).

John and Mary Gribbin, *The One Per Cent Advantage*, Oxford, Basil Blackwell, 1988
We wrote our two books in the wrong order – this one picks up where the one you are now holding ends.

John Gribbin and Jeremy Cherfas, *The Monkey Puzzle*, London, Paladin/Granada, 1983
An account of the development of the 'new', and now established, timescale of human development from the ape line.

Harry Harrison, *West of Eden*, London, Panther, 1985, and *Winter in Eden*, London, Grafton, 1986
The first two parts of a science fiction trilogy (part three 'coming soon') based on the idea that the dinosaurs were not wiped out 65 million years ago but continued to evolve and developed intelligence. Entertaining hokum with a smidgeon of evolutionary insight.

John Imbrie and Katherine Palmer Imbrie, *Ice Ages: Solving the Mystery,* London, Macmillan, 1979
A satisfyingly complete and enjoyably intelligible account of the development of what is known as the 'Milankovitch model' of ice ages, which explains how changes in the Earth's orientation in space produce climate cycles and ice age rhythms.

Donald Johanson and Maitland Edey, *Lucy: The Beginnings of Humankind,* London, Granada, 1981
The story of the discovery of the remains of the upright ancestor who represented either the first members of the human line after the split with the other apes, or the last common ancestors shared by people and other African apes.

Gwyn Jones, *A History of the Vikings,* Oxford University Press, 1968
Anything by Gwyn Jones on the Vikings is worth reading. This provides a wealth of background relevant to the Viking voyages discussed in chapter 6.

H. H. Lamb, *Climate, History and the Modern World,* London, Methuen, 1982
A *slightly* technical but still readable and very complete account of the influence of climate on human activities since the end of the latest ice age.

Jim Lovelock, *Gaia,* Oxford University Press, 1979
Jim Lovelock, *The Ages of Gaia,* Oxford University Press, 1988
If you are interested in the evolution of life on Earth, you must read these.

Roger Lewin, *Human Evolution,* Oxford, Basil Blackwell, 1984
The best 'instant guide' to the emergence of the human line, from a paleo-anthropological perspective.

Roger Lewin, *Bones of Contention,* New York, Simon and Schuster, 1987
A gossipy and entertaining account of the discoveries of fossil remains of our ancestors, and of the controversies surrounding those discoveries and their interpretation.

Milutin Milankovitch, *Durch ferne Welten und Zeiten,* Leipzig, Koehler & Amalang, 1936
OK, we really only put this one in to show off and impress anyone who doesn't read German. You're much better off getting the story of ice age cycles from the Imbries' book, unless you have a serious interest in the history of science and want it from the horse's mouth.

*H. G. Owen, *Atlas of continental displacement, 200 million years to the present,* Cambridge University Press, 1983
A gorgeous book which includes maps showing phases in the breakup of Pangea. The text is aimed at academics, but the maps are fascinating in their own right. Worth digging out of a library.

J. M. Roberts, *The Hutchinson History of the World,* London, Hutchinson, 1976
The best single-volume history of the world. Although Roberts does not acknowledge the importance of climatic change in helping to shape civilization, it is fascinating to compare the major developments he chronicles with the known pattern of climatic fluctuations, which we outline in this book and which are described in more detail by Hubert Lamb.

Carl Sagan, *The Dragons of Eden,* London, Coronet, 1978
Perhaps Sagan's best book; certainly his most provocative. Subtitled 'speculations on the evolution of human intelligence' – that sums it up.

Steven M. Stanley, *Extinction,* San Francisco, Scientific American Library, 1987
Crises for life on Earth, put in the perspective of climatic change and tectonic events. Beautifully illustrated, and authoritative. The best up-to-date account of the series of catastrophes that punctuates the evolutionary record of life on Earth.

G. Ledyard Stebbins, *Darwin to DNA, Molecules to Humanity,* San Francisco, W. H. Freeman, 1982
An up-to-date account of evolutionary ideas; non-technical but thorough.

*T. M. L. Wigley, M. J. Ingram and G. Farmer (eds), *Climate And History,* Cambridge University Press, 1981
Mainly for academics, this is the proceedings of a conference held at the University of East Anglia in 1979. Thomas McGovern's study of the Norse colony in Greenland is especially interesting; the whole book is worth dipping into in a library.

John Noble Wilford, *The Riddle of the Dinosaur,* New York, Knopf, 1985
A comprehensive overview of the dinosaur story, from the first discovery of dinosaur fossils to the controversies about disaster from space.

Index